# WOMEN AND THE SOCIAL REVOLUTION

Women And The Social Revolution


Spiderwize
Remus House
Coltsfoot Drive
Woodston
Peterborough
PE2 9BF
www.spiderwize.com
A CIP catalogue record for this book is available from the British Library.

ISBN: 978-1-912694-50-1
eBook ISBN: 978-1-912694-49-5

# WOMEN AND THE SOCIAL REVOLUTION

CLIFF SLAUGHTER,
VIVIEN SLAUGHTER
AND YASSAMINE MATHER

AND WITH AN ESSAY BY STEVE DRURY

EDITED BY CLIFF SLAUGHTER

SPIDERWIZE
Peterborough UK
2018

This book is dedicated to the memory of Maria Turner, the U.S. black woman who wrote in 1831, the year of Nat Turner's great rebellion against slavery:

*'O ye daughters of Africa, awake! awake! arise! no longer sleep nor slumber but distinguish yourselves. Show forth to the world that ye are endowed with noble and exalted faculties. How long shall the fair daughters of Africa be compelled to bury their minds and talents beneath a load of iron pots and kettles. How long shall a mean set of men flatter us with their smiles and enrich themselves with our hard earnings, their wives' fingers sparkling with rings and they themselves laughing at our folly?'*

# CONTENTS

Foreword ........ 1

**INTRODUCTION:**

Nothing To Lose But Your Chains ........ 3

**CHAPTER 1**

Women's Fight And Women's Plight ........ 9

**CHAPTER 2**

'Woman's Place'? Iraq, Turkey, Iran, Guatemala, France, Nazi Germany… ........ 19

**CHAPTER 3**

The Second Human Revolution ........ 31

**CHAPTER 4**

Our Humanitarian Crisis ........ 39

**CHAPTER 5**

'Class-Consciousness' And Women ........ 49

**CHAPTER 6**

A Mountain To Climb ........ 57

**CHAPTER 7**

What Does Anthropology Tell Us? ........ 71

Appendix ........ 75

**PART II**

Essays On Women's Emancipation ........ 83

# FOREWORD

In 2014, adapted productions of Sophocles' *Antigone*, and Euripides' *The Trojan Women* were staged in Beirut, then in Greece and in other European and Middle Eastern cities. Tabitha Ross wrote in *The Guardian:*

> *'State collapse from within, cities blown to rubble.' These lines from Sophocles' 2,400-year-old Greek play Antigone could have been written about Syria today... The play's director, Syrian Omar Abu Saada, says: 'The main theme of the text is a very important one for these women... insurgency, rebellion, disobedience... did they do right or wrong in deciding to ask for freedom?' This question has been endlessly discussed in rehearsals – both whether Antigone was right to insist on doing what she believes is moral despite the tragedy she brings, and whether the price Syrians are paying for challenging President Bashar al-Assad has been worth it, with 191,000 people killed and half the population driven from their homes.*
>
> (The Guardian, 10 December 2014.)

The truly remarkable fact about this is that the actors were Syrian women, witnesses and victims of the war in their homeland, with its mass murder, smashing and dispersal of families and communities, rape and torture. They found, in these wondrous achievements of Classical Greek civilisation over 2000 years ago, an echo of their own suffering at the hands of our modern barbarism, and, above all, a medium for confronting that barbarism and pointing the way to overcoming it.

A truly inspiring proclamation of hope and a clarion call for our time! Yes, if we are to move towards a future of freedom and equality, then women and men of our time will need to become conscious of and call up all the resources of human culture. Building upon these conquests and foundations, we shall see new generations living as free and equal individuals, building and rebuilding their own civilised communities.

INTRODUCTION:

# NOTHING TO LOSE BUT YOUR CHAINS

The emancipation of women is a demand which is elementary, basic and surely undeniable, and yet it is denied, necessitating the centuries-long struggle for women's liberation. That struggle has achieved real gains by way of concessions and reforms within the existing economic and political system. This system, the rule of capital, depends on exploitation and hierarchical domination, of men as well as women. It cannot exist without that exploitation and domination. So long as it exists, the liberation of women cannot be fully and finally achieved. The basic argument of this small book is that women's struggle for emancipation is at one with, and an indispensable part of, the fight to end the rule of capital, putting an end to exploitation and oppression of working people all over the world. The 'globalisation' of capital brings with it qualitatively new forms of interconnection and potential solidarity between the peoples of all countries. And the means of instant electronic communication, available to billions of people, provide the instruments of the 'universal intercourse' defined by Karl Marx as one of the essential prerequisites of a truly human, free and equal social existence. Thus the domination of a globalised capital destroying the lives of uncountable masses and even threatening the future of the planet at the same time now opens the door for a new and successful stage of the long struggle for freedom.

How is it possible, in this millennium, to start writing from any other standpoint than that of confrontation with the unprecedented humanitarian crisis created on a planetary scale by the 'globalised' capital system? The twentieth century saw the loss of millions of lives in Europe's two world wars, followed by carnage in the Far East, culminating in the genocidal bombing of Nagasaki and Hiroshima. And in Germany, Italy and Japan, equalled in brutality by the Stalinist regime in the Soviet Union, millions suffered under fascism. All that was already a grim confirmation of Rosa Luxemburg's warning at the beginning of the century, 'Socialism or Barbarism!' But today the humanitarian crisis is truly global. We are faced with a situation where parts of the world are in a state of virtually permanent war as the different sectors of capitalist power sacrifice innumerable lives in their search for geopolitical dominance and control of the world's natural resources. In these wars the displacement and scattering of millions of families, and the use of rape, are inhuman methods of social control and intimidation. In the meantime, obscene displays of wealth are shown among the upper classes in the richest and most powerful countries, while countless others suffer from poverty, hunger and starvation. The impending disaster hanging over all this is the ever-increasing threat of environmental destruction consequent on the uncontrolled imperative of capital accumulation. So-called neoliberalism, dominant since the late 1960s, provides for governments and corporate business the unapologetic and uncontrolled policy impetus for this (from the point of view of humanity and its future) disastrous course.

The central theme of this book is that the depth and breadth of this humanitarian crisis demands that every possible human resource must be summoned in order to confront and understand it, to fight to overcome its manifestations and to get rid of its causes.

Every human resource? Much has been written in the last century and a half about the correctness or incorrectness of Marx's conclusion that the working class is 'the gravedigger of capital'. And many feminist and other writers have argued that the liberation of women will finally be achieved only when the rule of capital is replaced, via a social (socialist) revolution, by a socialist society of free and equal individuals, so that women's fight should unite with the working-class movement for socialism. In addition, there is a long and honourable record of women fighters against poverty, war and oppression. In this book we give an account of these aspects. However, we present that account in the context of the question posed at the beginning of this introduction, namely, where are the human resources necessary to address, in ideas and in practice, our global humanitarian crisis?

On this basis, we maintain that in today's fight to eliminate the underlying cause of this humanitarian crisis, women are the great untapped and absolutely essential resource. Essential, because of their unique sensibility to the human suffering we see every day, a sensibility especially aroused by the fact that the methods of modern warfare and the extremes of poverty and starvation inflicted on millions have their major impact on women and children. (We shall repeat more than once that whether this sensibility derives from inborn qualities or social conditioning, or both, does not affect the argument.)

Why, then, is a central part of this book devoted to the question of working-class consciousness? Because in the light of what we have postulated on the role of women today, our understanding (our own and that of others) of that question requires radical revision. Too often, theories of class consciousness have neglected vital aspects. Women's part in past struggles has, until recently, often been ignored. More importantly, many of us have in the past stressed theoretical understanding of the necessity of revolution, but ignored the part played in revolutionary consciousness by feeling, passion, anger. And we will not understand or be armed to confront our present situation and the role of women in it, until that one-sidedness is corrected.

The title of this introduction is taken from the resounding call forming the closing words of the *Communist Manifesto*: *Die proletarian haben nichts zu verlieren als ihre Ketten. Sie haben eine Welt zu gewinnen. Proletarier aller Lander, vereinigt euch!* ('The proletarians have nothing to lose but their chains. They have a world to win. Proletarians of all lands, unite!') The usual English translation renders the last sentence:

'Working men of all countries, unite!' Given our starting point in this book, we need to say that the proletarians are working men and working women! Yes, unite!

As for 'nothing to lose but their chains', it became fashionable in the decades following the Second World War for sociologists and journalists in Western Europe and the US to write about 'the affluent worker', 'the consumer society', and even to declare 'we're all middle-class now'. And some Marxists (I include myself, CS) suggested that workers in the twentieth century had a good deal more to lose than their chains. This was true, but only in terms of material wellbeing, and only in the 'advanced' capitalist countries of the West. Now there are new considerations. Those material conditions, including and especially the reform concessions wrung from the ruling classes in the last century, are now being eroded, systematically undermined. Secondly, 'nothing to lose' has a new significance, as we have to live with the threat of destruction of the elementary natural and human conditions of a future society of free and equal men and women. This threat exists for the global population. And finally, we see a continuous series of humanitarian crises of unprecedented intensity. The nature of these crises underlines heavily the imperative necessity of grasping in theory and in practice the essential role of women in the working class's struggle to transform society.

The dangers which flow from the continued global rule of capital are growing by the day, as the 'great powers' thrash about, unavailingly and destructively, in search of a world order in which the resources of the planet, natural and geopolitical, can be controlled by capital without resistance, at whatever human cost.

Behind what is argued in the chapters which follow is a conviction that not all readers will share, namely, that against these deadly destructive dangers a social revolution is necessary. Our aim here is to correct the longstanding assumption, implicit or explicit, that this revolution is the job of men. The other half of the proletariat – that is, of the oppressed, propertyless and exploited of this world – are women. Without them, without their capacity for the feeling and passion aroused by the gigantic humanitarian crisis, there will be no solution, none of the solidarity needed for a social revolution, no anticipation theoretical or practical, of the future free and equal social order. Only as women assert their place in the struggle will there be a revival of the socially revolutionary role of the working class.

And this is a message also for men. Germaine Greer, pioneer of the fight to go beyond the earlier feminism(s), was driving at this when she wrote in *The Female Eunuch*:

> The first significant discovery we [women] shall make as we racket along our female road to freedom is that men are not free … By securing our own manumission we may show men the way that they could follow when they have jumped off their own treadmill. Privileged women will pluck at your sleeve and seek to enlist you in the 'fight' for reforms, but reforms are retrogressive. The old process must be broken, not made new. Bitter women will call you to rebellion, but you have too much to do. What will you do?
>
> (Germaine Greer, *The Female Eunuch*, Paladin, 1971, p.331.)

CHAPTER 1

# WOMEN'S FIGHT AND WOMEN'S PLIGHT

## SOME FAMOUS STRUGGLES BY WOMEN IN HISTORY

If Friedrich Engels was right in calling the origin of the male-dominated monogamous family 'the world-historical defeat of the female sex' (*The Origin of the Family, Private Property and the State*, Lawrence and Wishart, 1940, p.59), inseparable from and basic to the origin of private property and the state, then what are the implications of this for our assertion of women's role in the struggle for socialism, and in overcoming that defeat?

In front of the Parliament building in London there stand a statue of Emmeline Pankhurst and a plaque to Christabel Pankhurst, the state having chosen to commemorate their fight as suffragettes for votes for women, even though in the course of that fight more than a century ago this mother and daughter and their comrades were beaten, imprisoned and tortured by the forces of the same state. Christabel's sister Sylvia, who participated equally in the fight, has no such statue or plaque. Why? The establishment must have had its reasons. Yes. As late as 1948, by which time she was primarily involved in the anti-colonial movement, the security services were still monitoring her activities, and an MI5 file holds a memo stating that some way must be found of 'muzzling the tiresome Miss Sylvia Pankhurst'. (See: https://en.wikipedia.org/wiki/Sylvia_Pankhurst). Why was she thought so 'tiresome'?

Sylvia had been with her mother and sisters in founding the suffragette movement. Then in 1913 she founded the East London Federation of Suffragettes. At the same time she began a political and personal relationship with the socialist Keir Hardie. She worked to combine the fight for women's suffrage with the fight for socialism, looking for and finding support from working-class women and from the dockers of the area. Between February 1913 and August 1914 she was arrested eight times for her activities. Several times she had to be released from prison temporarily to recover from the effects of hunger-striking. Each time she was re-arrested women fought with police to defend her. She organised a people's army to defend suffragettes and striking dockers. She also organised many rent strikes in the same period.

Then, in August 1914, came the declaration of war with Germany. There was an immediate split in the suffragette movement. Emmeline Pankhurst and the Women's Social and Political Union (WPSU) negotiated with the Government, securing the release of all suffragettes by pledging to stop campaigning and support the war effort. Emmeline urged women 'to fight for their country as they fought for the vote …' But Sylvia was bitterly opposed, and with others formed the Women's Peace Army, later the Workers Suffrage Federation. With Dr Barbara Tchaikovsky she set up four mother-and-baby clinics in London.

In July 1917, Sylvia changed the name of the paper she had founded in March 1914 from *The Woman's Dreadnought,* to *The Workers' Dreadnought* with the slogan, 'Socialism, Internationalism, Votes for All', and when the October Revolution came, she enthusiastically supported it. Travelling to Russia, she met Lenin, and is said to have disagreed with him on the issue of censorship. On her return, her work in support of the revolution earned her a five month prison sentence for sedition.In 1920 Sylvia's organisation came together with several others, such as those led by Tom Bell, Arthur McManus, Harry Pollitt and J.T.Murphy, to found the Communist Party of Great

Britain. However, in 1924 she was expelled because of her refusal to hand over *The Workers' Dreadnought* to the control of the Party.

Sylvia Pankhurst fought for the rights of women and for the working class until her death in 1960. Outstanding were her support for the Republican fighters against Franco in Spain and against Mussolini in support of Ethiopia and Haile Selassie. Little wonder she has no statue in Parliament Square, and that MI5 found her 'tiresome'... This great woman knew that her fight for the rights of women meant she had to be a communist.

The year 2017 marked the centenary of the Russian revolution. The way in which it began is more than interesting:

> The 23rd of February [8 March – new style] was International Women's Day. The social-democratic circles had intended to mark this day in a general manner: by meetings, speeches, leaflets. It had not occurred to anyone that it might become the first day of the revolution. Not a single organisation called for strikes on that day. What is more, even a Bolshevik organisation, and a most militant one – the Vyborg borough-committee – all workers – was opposing strikes... Such was the course followed by the committee on the eve of the 23rd of February, and everyone seemed to accept it. On the following morning, however, in spite of all directives, the women textile workers in several factories went on strike, and sent delegates to the metal workers with an appeal for support. 'With reluctance,' writes Kayurov, 'the Bolsheviks agreed to this, and they were followed by the workers – Mensheviks and Social-Revolutionaries.'
>
> There followed the series of clashes with police and soldiers which eventually brought the February Revolution.
>
> (LD.Trotsky, *History of the Russian Revolution*, Victor Gollancz, 1936, p.123.)

In these clashes, a 'great role is played by women workers in the relation between workers and soldiers. They go up to the cordons more boldly than men, take hold of their rifles, beseech, almost command: "Put down your bayonets – join us"." *(Ibid.)* 'On February 23, under the flag of "Woman's Day", began the long-ripe and long-withheld uprising of the Petrograd working masses' (Trotsky, *op. cit.*, p 129).

In all the anti-colonial liberation struggles, in Asia, Africa and Latin America, women have taken up arms along with men. After the victory in Cuba, Fidel Castro acknowledged this role, but we surely cannot be satisfied with his further comment: 'Who will do the cooking for the child who still comes home for lunch? Who will nurse the babies or take care of the pre-school child? Who will cook for the man when he comes home from work? Who will wash and clean and take care of things?' Here we are, back again at 'woman's place is in the home.' (Barbara A. Crow, *Radical Feminism*, NYU Press, 2000, p.18.) One spokesman for black radical movements, Stokely Carmichael, put it more crudely: 'The only position for women in SNCC [Student Nonviolent Coordinating Committee] is prone.'(Sabina Peck, '"The Only Position for Women in SNCC is Prone": 'Stokely Carmichael and the Perceived Patriarchy of Civil Rights Organisations in America' in *History in the Making*, vol. I, 1: http://www.historyitm.org/index.php/hitm/article/view/19.)

The actions of women in February 1917 had spoken very differently. They were anticipated in the Paris Commune of 1871. Lissagaray, a participant, wrote the Commune's history. His chapter 'Our Parisiennes' describes a tableau in one of the Communard journals:

> In the streets, in the silent boulevards, a battalion of a hundred men setting out for the battle or returning from it; a woman who follows…The commander in his tunic, dusty, his silver lace singed, his men greyheads of youths, the veterans of June 1848 and the pupils of March, the son often marching by the side of the father.
>
> This woman, who salutes or accompanies them, she is the true Parisienne. The unclean androgyne, born in the mire of the Empire, the Madonna of the pornographers, the Dumas fils and

> the Feydaux, has followed her patrons to Versailles or works the Prussian mine at St. Denis. She, who is now uppermost, is the Parisienne, strong, devoted, tragic, knowing how to die as she loves. A helpmeet in labour, she will also be an associate in the death-struggle. A formidable equality this to oppose to the bourgeoisie. The proletariat is doubly strong – one heart and four hands.
>
> On the 24th of March a Federal addressed these noble words to the bourgeois battalions of the first arrondissement, making them drop their arms: 'Believe me, you cannot hold out; your wives are all in tears, and ours do not weep.'
>
> She does not keep back her husband. On the contrary, she urges him to battle, carries him his linen and his soup, as she had before to his workshop. Many would not return, but took up arms. At the plateau de Chatillon they were the last to stand the fire. The cantinières, simply dressed as workmen, no fancy costumes, fell by dozens. On the 3rd April, at Meudon, the Citoyenne Lachaise, cantinière of the 66th battalion, remained the whole day in the field of battle, tending the wounded, alone, without a doctor.
>
> (Prosper-Olivier Lissagaray, *History of the Commune of 1871*, International Publishing Company, New York, 1898, pp.207-8.)

A well-known example of women's part in revolutionary struggles is their participation in the Irish Easter Rising of 1916. CumannnamBan, the women's military organisation, had 200 members, including shop assistants, dressmakers, teachers, clerks, alongside artists, actresses and a doctor. Besides those bearing arms and participating in the fighting, there were many women risking their lives as 'basket girls'. One of the best known among the fighters was Margaret Skinnider, a primary school teacher in her twenties from Coatbridge, Scotland, who was wounded in April 1916, when commanding five men of the Irish Citizen Army on a mission to destroy houses in Harcourt Street, Dublin, to cut off enemy approaches. She was involved in the later Civil War, organising communications and the purchase of arms. She was also very active in the Irish National Teachers Organisation, fighting for equal pay for women, as were other women fighters from

1916 and the Civil War. Another 1916 fighter, the famous Countess Constance Markiewicz, who was in 1918 elected to the House of Commons, described women as 'the eyes and ears of the rebels.'

On the centenary of the Rising, writing in *The Observer* (27 March 2016) Ed Vulliamy cited extracts from hitherto unpublished letters written by Mabel, wife of Desmond Fitzgerald, one of the leaders of the Easter Rising. After describing the sufferings of women at the hands of the British soldiers, she wrote:

> You can see from this that the life of an Irish woman is not pleasant at the hands of the monsters the English people have loosed on us. Still, don't for an instant imagine that the women to whom these things happen, or those who are waiting for their turn, want to give in or are cowards, not a bit of it. The women are if possible firmer than the men and are going to the end which can only be victory. The spirit is great and every one is so used to suffering now, that there is no other course for the tyrant but to invent new indevilments, and these in the end must seal the doom of English rule.

In the history of trade union struggles there are hundreds of examples of the heroic part played by women workers. In Britain, in 1968, women machinists at the Ford Motor Company's Dagenham plant won a famous victory in their unofficial strike for equal pay and equal status with male workers. It was their struggle which led directly to the passing of the Equal Pay Act two years later. In 1970, clothing workers in Leeds, the great majority of them women, went on strike, spreading the action to every factory and organising picket lines. Despite the strike being declared unofficial by the union officials (as compellingly portrayed in *Leeds United*, a 1974 television play written by Colin Welland and directed by Roy Battersby) they were able to force major concessions in wage levels from the employers. More recently, the miners who went on a year-long strike against pit closures in 1984-5 were sustained by the highly organised miners' wives support groups before they were starved back to work, ironically by a very different woman – one whose actions make clear that the issue is not simply gender as such – Prime Minister Margaret Thatcher, who was determined to 'see off the miners', denouncing them and their families as 'the enemy within'.

Legendary in the history of women's trade union struggles is the 'Bread and Roses' strike of women workers in the United States in 1912. On 12 January in that year, 10,000 textile workers, most of them women, walked out of factories. These women were of several nationalities: Hungarian, Portuguese, French-Canadian, Syrian and Russian, as well as US American. Within a few days 25,000 were out on strike. Their demands were: a pay increase of 15 per cent; a 54-hour week; double pay for overtime; the elimination of bonus pay. Their banners read: 'We Want Bread, but Roses Too!' Organisers were called in from the IWW (International Workers of the World, known as 'the Wobblies'), including Elizabeth Gurley Flynn, Big Bill Haywood, William Trautmann and Carlo Tresca. There was support and aid in solidarity in all parts of the country.

On 29 January, picketing striker Anna La Pizza was shot dead. Against the protests and demonstrations aroused by this, martial law was declared. Hundreds of strikers' children were transported to New York. Children were forcibly taken from their mothers, some of whom were clubbed and beaten. But so solid was the strike that, on 12 March, the companies gave way to all the workers' demands.

For the next half-century Elizabeth Gurley Flynn continued relentlessly to fight for women's equality and for workers' rights. Her life's work was appropriately 'recognised' by the US Government in 1951, when she was arrested and charged under the Smith Act for 'conspiracy to overthrow the United States government.' She was found guilty as charged and imprisoned from 1955 to 1957.

## WOMEN IN REVOLUTIONARY STRUGGLES

Women's part in trade union and directly revolutionary struggles should come as no surprise. For countless centuries women have had to endure the most severe discrimination, exploitation and oppression, and have in many, many instances fought against that condition. Working people have for millennia, since the beginning of class society, been exploited and oppressed; the women of the working classes have been doubly exploited and oppressed because of male supremacy in the family. 'Galley slaves from birth' sums up their condition. Burdened with childbearing and child-rearing, these women have fought day in and day out, year after year, to sustain the lives of their families. Without that struggle, there would be no continuity of social life.

Here we should not be ensnared by the words 'social', society' and 'social function', as are many sociologists. The big question is: in our own type of society, one ruled by capital and its 'personification' as the ruling class, how does the family as a structure or institution, with its oppression of women, form an essential basis for the whole system of exploitation and oppression, and why does this give special significance to the role of women in the social revolution? Again Germaine Greer, going beyond the earlier feminisms:

> Women's liberation, if it abolishes the patriarchal family, will abolish a necessary substructure of the authoritarian state, and once that withers away Marx will have come true willy-nilly, so let's get on with it. Let the men distribute leaflets in factories where the proletariat have become hire-purchase slaves instead of communists.... Women represent the most oppressed class of life-contracted unpaid workers, for whom slaves is not too melodramatic a description. They are the only true proletarians left...
>
> (Greer, *The Female Eunuch*, pp.368-9)

In its own way, this echoes the verdict of Marx and Engels in the *Communist Manifesto*:

> The bourgeois claptrap about the family and education, about the hallowed co-relation of parents and child, becomes all the more disgusting, the more, by the action of modern industry, all the family ties among the proletarians are torn asunder, and their children transformed into simple articles of commerce and instruments of labour.
>
> But you Communists would introduce community of women, screams the bourgeoisie in chorus.
>
> The bourgeois sees his wife a mere instrument of production. He hears that the instruments of production are to be exploited in common, and, naturally, can come to no other conclusion than that the lot of being common to all will likewise fall to the women.
>
> He has not even a suspicion that the real point aimed at is to do away with the status of women as mere instruments of production...
>
> Our bourgeois, not content with having wives and daughters of the proletarians at their disposal, not to speak of common prostitution, take the greatest pleasure in seducing each other's wives.
>
> Bourgeois marriage is, in reality, a system of wives in common... It is self-evident that the abolition of the present system of production must bring with it the abolition of the community of women springing from that system, i.e., of prostitution, both public and private.

In later chapters we take up the question of why the socialist revolution is, as Marx insisted, a 'human revolution'. The relations between women and men will be a decisive test of that thesis.

> The direct, natural and necessary relation of person to person is *the relation of man to woman*. In this natural species-relationship man's relation to nature is immediately his relation to man, just as his relation to man is immediately his relation to nature – his own natural destination. In this relationship, therefore, is *sensuously*

*manifested*, reduced to an observable *fact*, the extent to which the human essence has become nature to man, or to which nature to him has become the human essence of man.

(Karl Marx, *Economic and Philosophical Manuscripts of 1844* in Marx and Engels, *Collected Works* [*MECW*], vol. 3, Lawrence and Wishart, 1975, p. 296; the full passage is discussed below, in chap. 5.)

CHAPTER 2

# 'WOMAN'S PLACE'? IRAQ, TURKEY, IRAN, GUATEMALA, FRANCE, NAZI GERMANY...

In the harsh light of the fate of women in our 'globalised' world today, a truly liberated future inevitably seems utopian. Examples of this fate are before our eyes every day: we mention only a fraction here. For example, in just one day (11 September 2016) in *The Guardian* newspaper, we could read the following articles. First, a feature on Yazidi women, shown in the work of photographer Alfred Yaghobzadeh:

> Islamic State sees all Yazidis as pagan infidels. In August 2014, Isis attacked Yazidi villages in the Sinjar region of Iraq, driving locals into the mountains. They bulldozed villages, captured thousands of women as sex slaves and slaughtered everyone in their path, transforming the area into a terrorised war zone....
>
> Yaghobzadeh took partial portraits of women who were kidnapped, tortured and raped by Isis, subjected to 'everything you could imagine for women among savages.' On top of the trauma, most deny they were raped because of the culture of shame around sex (young women often say their friends were, but that they were not)...
>
> One such picture is of a 15-year-old girl called Gulan closing her eyes and covering her face with her hand, her pink nail polish a gut-

> wrenching sign of ordinary youth in unfathomable circumstances. Last year, her family was killed and she spent two months in the hands of Isis. She told Yaghobzadeh the only sense of relief she felt was when she was beaten.
>
> His main focus is on the local military, which is now all but run by women... Though it is the first all-female brigade of Yazidi fighters, there are precedents nearby. The YPJ (Kurdish Women's Protection Unit) and YPG (People's Protection Unit) are the armed branches of a Kurdish coalition in northern Syria, and have thousands of volunteer fighters, both men and women. There is a YPJ/YPG subset in Sinjar, who played a crucial role in rescuing Yazidis trapped by Isis on Mount Sinjar in 2014, along with the PKK (Kurdish militant organisation founded on revolutionary Marxism) and the Peshmerga (Kurdish fighters in Iraq).
>
> It's a survivalist and egalitarian coalition: men and women are fighting the same battle here. They've lost everything, but they're determined to be useful to their community. The women are always on standby and in uniform; they sleep in it, and they sleep in their shoes. 'And they will be in their uniform until they get what they want – independence,' says Yaghobzadeh. This sense of resilience and retribution becomes even more revolutionary in a military context: 'For Isis it's a harem. If you're killed by a woman, you don't go to paradise....The most important and sensitive position – facing Isis – is in the hands of women,' he says. 'Women are always the victim: in the West, in the East, in the Middle East.' But here, 'each one has a reason to fight and survive. They know they're deciding their own life.'

And second, on Turkey:

> In 2015, Turkey's constitutional court announced that civil marriage would no longer be required for couples who were married in a religious ceremony. This... made it easier for families to marry off their daughters before they reached the legal age. The outcries of women's organisations have been ignored. The ministry of women and family was turned into the ministry of family and

> social policy. The dropping of the word 'women' was more than symbolic. Turkey is increasingly becoming more conservative and patriarchal, and a harder place for women's rights.
>
> Since the Syrian crisis erupted, the number of child brides has escalated. An alarming number of Turkish men are marrying Syrian women as their second or third wives. Even though polygamy is illegal in Turkey, the practice is not discouraged. Nezahat Bolge, a woman's rights advocate and lawyer, says Syrian girls aged 15 and 16 are married to 50- and 60-year-old Turkish men as their second wives. 'Some of these girls are married in return for a golden bracelet or ring,' says a jeweller in Kilis, a city near the Syrian border. Across Turkey, domestic violence continues to spiral. Although a recent government report admitted that around 40 per cent of Turkish women experience sexual violence, the [ruling] AKP does not see the fight against gender violence as a priority...The increase in religious fanaticism goes hand in hand with an increase in sexism.

Meanwhile the European governments ignore all of this and play suitor to Erdogan's authoritarian regime in search of some 'solution' to what they call their(!) refugee and asylum crisis. In the pursuit of their 'war on terror', they of course ignore also the fact that it is the West's recent role in Iraq, Saudi Arabia and the whole of the Middle East, not to mention centuries of colonial exploitation and support of military and other reactionary regimes, which have fuelled the rise of Islamist fundamentalism and lie at the root of all these atrocities.

The London *Times* reported the following on 10 March 2016:

> An Iranian MP has provoked outrage after insisting that women, like donkeys, have no place in parliament... 'The parliament is not the place for babies and donkeys. The parliament is no place for women. The parliament is for men,' Mr Qazipour claimed as his predominantly male supporters cheered.
>
> Mr Qazipour went on to warn that female MPs would distract their male counterparts and entice them into shameful sexual liaisons. Homosexuals should also be excluded from parliament, he said.

And so on, ad nauseam.

Mr Qazipour's views are certainly not exceptional in Iran. As Yassamine Mather explains:

> Since the establishment of the Islamic republic in 1979 the plight of Iranian women has worsened, the rigid imposition of the veil (hijab) has reinforced discrimination and prejudice against women. Many families refuse to send their daughters to high school. In higher education girls are discouraged or prevented by the state from studying or working in fields and activities considered 'masculine', such as engineering, mining, the judiciary … it is in opposition to the state that many women pursue such studies.
>
> There is discrimination against women in sport and recreation. Participation in some sports is discouraged, and in recreation most facilities are rigidly segregated and rarely available to women. Many have called this a system of apartheid against women. The ministry of education in the Iranian government recently reported that 94 per cent of schoolgirls were unfit, as they did not participate in sport or physical education.
>
> The combination of enforced hijab wearing and segregation is used to limit women's access to state education, sports and other facilities. In other words, the system is geared to institutionalise women's confinement to the home…
>
> As they become teenagers, girls are driven more and more into a world dominated and manipulated by their male relatives. They can be given away in legal marriage without their knowledge or consent while still in their childhood. The legal age of marriage for girls is nine.
>
> The law discriminates against women in inheritance, giving them at most half of the share of their male counterparts. According to the laws of Hodud and Qessas (making the punishment correspond to the crime), the life of a woman is worth half that of a man, with the implication that a man killing a woman and

> sentenced to death may only be executed if the victim's family pays the murderer half of his death dues. Article 6 of this law states that the bereaved family has to pay the murderer's family to get 'Islamic justice' (a life for a life)…
>
> Islamic marriage laws as applied in Iran are amongst the most repressive in the world in terms of discrimination against women. While men are allowed to marry up to four wives at a time in permanent marriage, plus an unlimited number of women in what is known as 'temporary marriage (siqeh)', women who do not adhere to strict monogamy are considered criminal and may be brutally and savagely stoned to death in public. This legal Islamic punishment for extra-marital affairs is carried out regularly in Iran.
>
> Men control the lives of their wives, their daughters and their unmarried sisters. In Islamic societies women need a male guardian throughout their lives, to give them legal permission to travel, to study, to marry, etc… As no consent is required for sexual relations inside marriage, wife-rape is common and even wife-beating is tolerated in the process (with a Qur'anic verse that legitimises wife-beating in the case of 'disobedient women'). Abortion is illegal, but the rising number of terminations is testimony to its use as a form of contraception.
>
> (Yassamine Mather in *Weekly Worker*, 24 December 2015)

As long ago as 8 March 1979, International Women's Day, Iranian women had asserted their right to freedom. Tens of thousands of them took part in the first major demonstration against the newly established Islamic Republic, following the forced imposition of the hijab. The women's slogans were: 'I say it every moment, I say it under torture: either death or freedom!' 'Freedom is neither eastern nor western: it is universal!' 'In the dawn of freedom, the place of women is empty: revolution is meaningless without women's freedom – we do not want the hijab!'

In Guatemala, it was reported on 2 March 2016:

> In a landmark ruling the Supreme Court has sentenced two men to lengthy prison sentences for the systematic rape of 15 indigenous women during the 1990s. After 20 days of dramatic testimony, a retired army officer and a former paramilitary were convicted of sexually enslaving 15 indigenous women during the country's civil war… Heriberto Valdez Asij was jailed for 240 years for crimes against humanity and the forced disappearance of seven of the women's husbands. Lieutenant-Colonel Esteelmer Reyes Giron was sentenced to 120 years in jail for crimes against humanity and the murder of 20-year-old Cuc Coc and her two daughters ….
>
> Cuc Coc's husband was killed, but she and her children managed to flee into the mountains until they could no longer endure the dire conditions. 'We went to the military base and got on our knees and begged them to forgive us, to not kill us,' she said in her recorded testimony. 'Many times I was raped. One of my daughters was raped too. Every day I suffer because of what they did to us.'…
>
> DemeciaYat de Xol explained how she was raped at home and then forced to live in the camp for months as punishment for searching for her disappeared husband. 'They put us (women) in a room and began raping us. I was pregnant at the time and suffered a miscarriage.'
>
> Yat also testified that her cousin Dominga Cuc was locked in a small house at the base and raped by soldiers until she was 'practically lifeless'. 'I don't know who gave the order but we could hear the shooting, then we heard that she had been killed,' she said.

Judge Yassmin Barrios concluded: 'It is a way to attack the country, killing or raping victims. Women were seen as a military objective.' (Nina Lakham, in *The Guardian*, 2 March 2016)

Such extremes, of which thousands could be cited, have their precedents in the history of brutal regimes and armies which plundered and raped ever since the medieval era.They have roots in the ideological and practical versions of keeping women in 'woman's place'. They are matched by the flood of revelations of sexual abuse which engulfed Britain in the second decade of this century, much of which was highly organised, many involving 'celebrities', many reaching to the establishment, most of them ignored and concealed by the police and the criminal justice system. All this after centuries of the criminalisation of abortion, condemnation of prostitution public and domestic, and inequality and discrimination for women in every sphere of life.

Under French rule in Vietnam:

> Women were recruited, often by force, into plantations, mines, and factories. Between 1917 and 1945, 16 per cent of the 280,000 workers on three large rubber plantations were officially reported to have died; more died unreported. By 1945, 60 per cent of the plantation workers were women. Factory hands worked a fifteen-hour day, seven days a week. The women sometimes gave birth on the factory floor, afraid to lose their jobs if they reported sick. In the 1940s, 30 per cent of women who died, died in childbirth, and the infant mortality rate was between 30 and 40 per cent. Women factory workers in the 1930s were paid one-fifth of the wages of men, sometimes less. In famine years women sold themselves, or were sold, into slavery or concubinage for a few pounds of rice. Women who protested against their conditions were placed in head stocks, jailed, tortured, or executed. French administrators admitted that there were 'three prisons for every school'.
>
> (Kathleen Gough, *Ten Times More Beautiful: The Rebuilding of Vietnam*, Monthly Review Press, 1978, pp.78-79)

Vietnam's feudal rulers had held to the contemporary Chinese adage: 'One hundred women are not worth a single testicle'; in the spirit of which, the French colonial administration in Cochinchina issued a decree which included the sentence, 'The woman is represented by her husband in all affairs concerning her.' (Ibid.)

The fascist regimes of twentieth-century Germany and Italy were notorious in their explicit suppression of women. But this was only an extreme and finished expression of the way in which women are exploited and oppressed in capitalist societies. On the eve of the Second World War against Nazi Germany, the Daladier regime in France put in place its 'Family Code' (July 1939):

> Ten-year jail sentences for convicted abortionists, cash incentives for couples who had a child within the first two years of marriage, the abandonment of partible inheritance, and the adoption of marriage loans for young farmers to reverse migration from the countryside. Vichy perpetuated these policies, with endless rhetoric about the family as *'la cellule essentielle'*. Divorce laws were tightened, with divorce prohibited during the first three years of marriage, under a law of April 1941... Women were expelled from certain professions and given an educational diet of cooking and housekeeping. Motherhood was not only regarded as a duty to the state and hence feted, if not rewarded, but was interpreted as essential to the psychological health of women, 'for if there is anything sadder than a garden without flowers... it is a woman without children'.
>
> (Michael Burleigh, *The Third Reich, a New History*, Macmillan, 2000, p.470)

> Women's magazines gave extended coverage of film stars talking to a laughing Führer on the telephone or admiring the exhibits at the Automobile Show, and to the wives and children of other Nazi leaders. Women's magazines included photographs of the coffee breaks enjoyed by the grateful inmates of concentration camps, amid the racially vetted models and tips on household management. Since slush knows no national boundaries, it is unsurprising that in 1938 Ignatius Phayre of the British *Homes and Gardens* profiled Hitler and his cacti in majolica pots at Berchtesgarden, reassuring British readers that Hitler was 'a droll raconteur' and that the *caneton a la presse* and the *truitesaumon a la Monseigneur* were passable.
>
> (Burleigh, op. cit.,p.209)

The reality for women under this 'droll' dictator was very different from what Phayre's readers might have imagined.

> In 1938 the Nazis instituted Mothers' Crosses in bronze, silver and gold for women 'rich in children'. The French Superior Council for Natality had been doing this since 1920.... The selection criteria were designed to distinguish laudable, independent and orderly families 'rich in children' from unworthy, dependent and dysfunctional 'large families'.... Women who produced children serially with different partners were ineligible. So too were Jews and Gypsies, who were disqualified from awards which were designed to enhance respect for mothers in society, and from which preferential treatment ensued...

As for Hitler,

> On the one hand the desperately conventional figure doting on little boys and girls, scoffing cream cakes, in an atmosphere of forced gaiety; on the other a brooding warlord, more taken with smouldering cities under blue-grey, smouldering skies. His emotional range only covered the former. Bearers of Mothers' Crosses soon discovered that the most acceptable child of all was he who fell for the Motherland, for which double sacrifice they received these analogues of military decorations... This conflation of birth and violent death, so symptomatic of the adolescent, death-fixated, kitschy sensibility informing Nazi politics, was explicit in poetry:
>
> Mothers, your cradles,
> Are like a slumbering army
> Ever ready for victory
> They will be empty never more
>
> (Burleigh, op.cit., p.232.)

Hitler himself pronounced the doctrine behind such policies: 'Liberalism has a large number of points for women's equality. The Nazi programme for women has but one: this is the child. While man makes his supreme sacrifice on the field of battle, woman fights her supreme battle for her nation when she gives birth to a child.' This definition of gender roles was firmly embedded in Nazi racist ideology. Richard Brady wrote in his *The Spirit and Structure of German Fascism* (Left Book Club, Gollancz, 1937, p.187), quoting from Rudolf Hess and F.L.Schumann:

> When she fulfils her nature-allotted roles properly, she will gain the respect which is due to her as an embodiment of German womanhood.... The German woman who is bred in a true National-Socialist sense to be a German mother ... [will not be the] 'Gretchen type', [but rather] ... a woman intellectually capable to stand by her husband in his interests and his struggle with life and make his life richer and fuller ... Every Aryan hero should marry only a blonde Aryan woman with blue, wide-open eyes, a long and oval face, a pink and white skin, a narrow nose, a small mouth, and under all circumstances virginal. A blond blue-eyed Aryan hero must marry no brunette, no Mediterranean-type woman with short legs, black hair, hooked nose, full lips, a large mouth, and an inclination to plumpness. A blond blue-eyed Aryan hero must marry no Negroid type of woman with the well-known Negroid head and thinnish body. The Aryan hero must marry his equal Aryan woman, but not one who goes out too much or likes theatres, entertainment, or sport, or who cares to be seen outside her house.

And so the Nazis understood very well that old nostrum, not at all confined to Germany, 'woman's place is in the home'.

> When one says that the man's world is the State, his struggle, his preparation for solidarity, then one may perhaps say that the woman's world is a smaller one – her world is her husband, her family, her children and her home... what would become of the greater world, if there were no one to tend and care for the smaller one? The greater world is built upon the very foundation of this smaller world. The two worlds are not antagonistic – they

complement one another, they belong together just as husband and wife belong together.

(Hitler, speaking to the Women's Congress at Nuremberg, September 1934. See German History in Documents and Images: http://ghdi.ghi-dc.org/sub_document.cfm?document_id=1557)

'Woman's place is in the home' is no more than the vulgar and naïve expression of, and apology for, the fact that:

the family is the true microcosm of society, fulfilling beyond its immediate functions also the requirements of securing the continuity of property, to which we must also add its role as the basic unit of distribution and its unique ability to act as the 'transmission belt' of the prevailing value-structure of society. [For these reasons] the cause of women's liberation directly or indirectly affects the totality of social relations, in all their untenability'. (István Mészáros, *BeyondCapital,* Merlin Press, 1995, p.687.)

Women's plight, past and present, and their fight against it in many different forms, take us to the heart of what is argued in the chapters that follow. The fearsome humanitarian crisis caused by globalised capital's structural crisis hits women hardest of all, and it must arouse the sensibilities of which women are especially capable. And here is the source of a leap forward in that solidarity which is so central to any revolutionary advance. Germaine Greer was driving at an essential truth when she wrote that women are 'the only true proletarians left'. They are doubly exploited and doubly oppressed. More than working men, and on the global scale more and more every day, 'they have nothing to lose but their chains'. 'Imperative need' is indeed the necessary trigger for truly revolutionary action. We now have before us the imperative needs, not of this or that individual woman or group of women, but of the countless millions suffering from the misery of war, displacement, homelessness, their images placed before our eyes every day by the media.

CHAPTER 3

# THE SECOND HUMAN REVOLUTION

We can say that so far as relations of dominance between the sexes is concerned, as in every other way, the 'dehumanisation' which has always been one side of life in class society (in particular of course for the exploited classes) reaches its very depths in capitalism, where use-value is subordinated to exchange-value, productive labour subordinated to the accumulation of value (and the self-expansion of capital), the worth of an individual reduced to his/her usefulness in rendering surplus value to an alien power, capital.

In the socialist society which follows capitalism, the monogamous family will no longer be required as the reproductive framework for the commodity labour-power or the inheritance of private property. Production will be the production of use-values by free individuals as participants in the working of the 'social brain'. How these individuals will be reared and formed will be an entirely new question, to be taken up by free men and women. As Lewis Henry Morgan concluded in 1877:

> When the fact is accepted that the family has passed through four successive forms, and is now in a fifth, the question at once arises whether this form can be permanent in the future. The only answer that can be given is that it must advance as society advances, and change as society changes, even as it has done in the past. It is the creature of the social system, and will reflect its

> culture. As the monogamian family has improved greatly since the commencement of civilisation, and very sensibly in modern times, it is at least supposable that it is capable of still further improvement until the equality of the sexes is obtained. Should the monogamian family in the distant future fail to answer the requirements of society, assuming the continuous progress of civilisation, it is impossible to predict the nature of its successor.
>
> (Morgan, *Ancient Society*, Bharati Library, Calcutta, Part III, n.d., p.499.)

Morgan was just as enlightened on the question of the nature of the 'society of the distant future':

> A mere property career is not the final destiny of mankind, if progress is to be the law of the future as it has been of the past. The time which has passed away since civilisation began is but a fragment of the past duration of man's existence: and but a fragment of the ages yet to come. The dissolution of society bids fair to become the termination of a career of which property is the end and aim; because such a career contains the elements of self-destruction. Democracy in government, brotherhood in society, equality in rights and privileges and universal education, foreshadow the next higher plane of society to which experience, intelligence and knowledge are steadily tending. It will be a revival, in a higher form, of the liberty, equality and fraternity of the ancient gentes (Morgan, *op. cit.*, p.561).

*Homo sapiens* is physically unique, as is every other species, but our relation to nature, our mode of staying alive, is qualitatively different from that of any other species. It is not regulated by inherited, automatic, instinctive exchanges with the rest of nature. The necessary physical, biological, chemical exchanges with nature are achieved through social labour. The daily reproduction of life depends on this labour. It is *social* labour, i.e. the means and methods of doing it are not individual but require a system of relations between individuals and a historically acquired culture (in particular a division of labour), a mode of production.

The transition to the human required certain physical, biological, genetic advances (erect posture, opposable finger and thumb, thin cranium, a more complex brain with greatly increased learning capacity, etc.). The human child needs maternal care for a much longer time than in other species, which has obvious implications for a certain kind of domestic life and family. Archaeological discoveries show us that the using and making of tools occur in a social context. For the means of communication (language and ritual) essential for the social and cultural existence unique to our species to come into being, much larger brains, capable of a new kind of consciousness, were of course essential.

In this process, the role of women was of course different from that of men. Not only are human offspring incapable of independent activity and self-preservation for far longer than are the offspring of any other species; several years of childcare are necessary for learning to take shape. Food-gathering by women was an essential role from the beginning, but in the climatic conditions of the onset of the last Ice Age in which modern humanity emerged (the Upper Palaeolithic in Europe, some 100,000 years earlier in Africa), diet had to be supplemented by meat, and that meant that mothers and their children must have a settled social relationship with males, who were free from the responsibilities of childcare and hunted big game. These early humans learned to live in settled rather than nomadic conditions (the evidence suggests both existed), in small communities based on common matrilineal descent – matrilineal clans or 'gentes' (singular 'gens').

Exogamy (procreation outside the clan) and a ban on incest were the rules – migrants from Africa to Europe would have been small, isolated bands: as for incest, the line may have been drawn differently – siblings, parents, first cousins? There had to be solidarity and controlled sharing by the members of these descent-groups (not individual bargains of individual women with individual males). This revolution, as well as the ability to use and develop advanced stone tools, was essential to the establishment of truly human society and culture, overcoming a simply animal interchange with nature. Now there had to be cultural continuity, achieved at that early stage by ritual and society-wide codified systems of kinship and descent.

This cultural continuity, this solidarity, community and equality, were at the very root of 'becoming human'. They have to be revived in the higher forms made possible by millennia of our ancestors' achievements, in a new 'human revolution' to overcome the dehumanisation now inflicted on us by the rule of capital.

For hundreds of thousands of years, even two million, these social systems based on kinship and territorial groupings survived, adapting subsistence production to varied environments and natural resources and with a wide variety of forms of social organisation. They gave way, with the development of agriculture and livestock herding in especially favourable conditions, to the possibility of production of a surplus, and thus to societies with private property, the state, social classes and the exploitation of man by man. The archaeological record shows that it is only some 6,000 years ago that such societies were firmly established, first in the Middle East, and by 3,000 years ago on all inhabited continents except Australia.

With private property and the imperative of its being inherited came the beginning of the male-dominated monogamous family and the oppression of women. The fundamental humanity of the first 'human revolution' came under permanent attack, with exploitation of the direct producers and the subordination of women in the patriarchal family. Since then, 'the history of all societies has been the history of class struggle'.

In the last of these class-divided societies, capitalism, the social nature of production develops to the point where it comes into extreme contradiction with private property in the means of production and the exploitation of the direct producers. And here we arrive at that 'socialisation of production' so central to Marx's ideas. Every act of labour calls into play the body of knowledge and practice of society, the 'social brain', even though the resources of this brain are appropriated and commanded piecemeal as fixed capital, when they patently require social control.

This collective control will restore a relation of humans to the rest of nature which nurtures nature, not exploits it, and which nurtures humans and their relations with each other, instead of exploiting them. And so, once more, the socialist revolution is not the replacement of one form of class rule by another, but the human revolution, just as was the first human revolution (at the origin of human society and culture). Just as then, the freedom of women is central to it.

The 'human revolution' that made possible community and culture was eventually followed by the transition to the nuclear family dominated by the male, together with private property. This 'world historical defeat of the female sex' (Engels) can be called 'counter-revolutionary' (negation of the first human revolution). Capitalism is the last of the class societies which resulted. Today, among the pathological results of capitalism's overdevelopment are the commodification of sex and the illusory freedom of divorce and multiple relationships. The nuclear family, embedded in the dominance of men, is breaking up, and the broken-up men and women find themselves in a world where society is not community, and there remain only fragmentary communities (whereas the first human revolution embedded sexual relations in community).

The conditions for the abolition of want and for mutual cooperation have matured, indeed overdeveloped, and the contradiction between this socialisation of production and the capitalist mode of production endangers humanity. Just as a revolution – the first human revolution – was necessary in order for 'society to organise sex' and achieve the beginning of culture, so now another revolution is necessary to restore society's self-control and the equality of women and men. As in the original human revolution, it will require the organisation and collective consciousness of men and women to overcome the contradictions we have described and to build the new order. The first human revolution overcame the conflict with nature. As suggested in Steve Drury's essay below, this revolution proceeded as an immensely prolonged interaction between developing consciousness and constantly changing ecosystems in which humans actually changed their physiology to go beyond the purely natural. The second human revolution, the social revolution, will have a very different dynamic, involving a higher form of consciousness: wide and complex, but of course not complete, knowledge; previously unimaginable means of production; opposition to threats both environmental and those coming from the rule of global capital; in consequence, practical consciousness of the necessity of class struggle.

The liberation of women will be more than the accumulation of equal rights with men within the existing social, economic and political system. (Some of the limits of such gains are suggested by the 'right' of women to aspire to or achieve political leadership: the abhorrent Margaret Thatcher? or Marine Le Pen? or the murderous Winnie Mandela?) Women's liberation will be an essential part of the liberation of all humans.

To summarise on the 'second human revolution':

> [Ever since the dissolution of the primeval communal ownership of land] all history has been a history of class struggles, of struggles between exploited and exploiting, between dominated and dominating classes at various stages of historical development. This struggle, however, has now reached a stage where the exploited and oppressed class (the proletariat) can no longer emancipate itself from the class which exploits and oppresses it (the bourgeoisie), without at the same time for ever freeing the whole of society from exploitation, oppression and class struggles – this thought belongs solely and exclusively to Marx.
>
> (See Engels' prefaces to the 1883 German and the 1888 English editions of the Communist Manifesto.)

This dissolution of the primeval communal ownership of land (effectively, several human variants shared three continents for most of prehistoric time) brought with it private property in the means of production and the beginning of the state as property's protector and controller of the exploited majority. It bought also the patrilineal, male-dominated monogamous family as the assurance of inherited property. This origin of the modern family Engels famously called 'the world-historical defeat of the female sex'. The whole transformation can be seen as the negation of what went into the struggle to 'become human'. And now, the social revolution to overcome private property in the means of production, to begin the process of the 'withering away of the state' and put society in control of our own destiny instead of its being ruled by the needs of capital, will be the negation of that negation. It will restore, at an entirely new and higher level, the equality and classlessness of the order achieved in the first human revolution.

This is one way of understanding the content of Marx's insistence that the (proletarian) socialist revolution is the human revolution. Every previous revolution had replaced the rule of one exploiting class by that of another, rising, exploiting class; but the working class has no mode of exploitation of its own which it seeks to impose. In freeing itself from exploitation by capital, it must end exploitation as such, thus acting in the interest of all humanity. This second human revolution, when it puts to an end the exploitation of one class by another, an end to private property in the means of production and subjection of human life to the imperatives of capital, an end to state oppression, will be negating at the same time that 'world-historical defeat of the female sex'. The liberation of women will be achieved, and will be at the core of, this social revolution, this second human revolution.

From this historical standpoint, we surely must strive to see a way beyond women's struggles, many of them heroic, for reforms and rights which leave essentially intact the existing social order. Like all struggles for reforms, they have their real importance only insofar as they educate, prepare and mobilise the class for social revolution. We need also to go beyond the view which sees women as no more than an auxiliary to the revolutionary struggles of men. Women have an unconditionally central role in the preparation and process of the social revolution, and we have entered a stage in which the historical (structural, not merely conjunctural) crisis of the capital system, is now openly manifest as a global humanitarian disaster, where that role must and will come into its own.

CHAPTER 4

# OUR HUMANITARIAN CRISIS

> Perhaps the plight of our society has become so desperate and so apparent that women can no longer be content to leave it to other people.
>
> (Greer, *The Female Eunuch*, p.15.)

It is almost 100 years since Walter Benjamin warned that it was necessary to stop thinking in terms of the previous (nineteenth) century. And now we need to avoid seeing our situation in twentieth-century terms, even though it was an 'epoch of wars and revolutions', two of those wars being world wars costing millions of lives, and Rosa Luxemburg's words in 1903 – 'socialism or barbarism!' – ringing true throughout the century. Today we do not experience a day without war. This state of affairs and the accompanying horrific humanitarian crisis globally have their roots in the structural crisis – economic, social, political and moral – of the capital system.

For more than a century and a half it has been a fundamental tenet of socialist theory, derived from Marx, that capitalism and its dynamic was unwittingly creating the material conditions for the future socialist society, i.e., advanced productive forces and the means of universal intercourse. But today the same dynamic of self-reproduction of capital has become a predominantly destructive self-reproduction (Mészáros). It is destructive of the elementary material foundations (even threatening the planet's very existence) of a future society of free and equal human beings, and it is destructive of today's human beings. We are bombarded by countless examples of this inhumanity every day by media with global reach and immediate coverage.

And here there is a new contradiction. The means of production and the means of communication more and more coincide. On one side, the processes of production tend more and more to be programmed and executed by computer systems. On the other, the 'universal intercourse', the beginnings of which Marx perceived, is now infinitely more developed, most of all because of electronic communication and the 'information revolution'. While it is true that these means of communication give great advantages to capital in production and in control of information and ideological conditioning, they are now at the same time available to many millions of ordinary people, and potentially to everyone. This has positive and quite unprecedented implications for organising against capitalist exploitation and oppression, and on the necessary global scale. It is a revolutionary consequence of what Marx called 'the conquest of space by time'.

Against this background, the daily recurring human disasters and the fate of millions of people forced into an exodus into Europe have aroused strong feelings of sympathy and anger. Such feelings, and not only a reasoned understanding of the causes and necessary remedy of the situation, are an integral component of the consciousness (class-consciousness) and action necessary for the second human revolution, just as they were for the first, which took mankind beyond a merely natural, animal existence. The feelings of empathy aroused by the consequences of capitalist oppression and exploitation are a vast, untapped resource for the 'revolutionising practice' of the oppressed and exploited. And let us not forget: 'In modern warfare, women and children on the ground are in greater danger than the professionals who maim and kill them from a distance.' (Germaine Greer, *The Whole Woman*, Doubleday, 1999, p.164). It is surely not necessary to describe here the horrors of the Syrian civil war, the displacement of millions of families, and the fate of those millions who had the resources to try to escape by migrating to Europe, nor the African mass poverty and malnutrition leading to death by starvation, which weigh most of all on mothers and their children.

Restricting ourselves to the condition of women in this humanitarian crisis, we must not forget the sexual persecution of millions of women. There could be no more compelling example of the decadence and dehumanisation characterising the stage reached by capital's decline and crisis, recalling vividly Rosa Luxemburg's 'socialism or barbarism'. No apologies for this lengthy list of examples:

> Sandy beaches, turquoise waters... the picture of paradise. The Kenyan coast offers some of the most beautiful locations for people to relax and enjoy their free time. Sadly, the reality for almost one in three young girls is one where tourists visit the coast and single them out for commercial sexual exploitation. It is estimated that before the age of 12 almost 30 per cent of girls are already exploited for transactional sex along the coast, fuelled by the tourists who visit Kenya for that very reason.
>
> (See http:// www.ecpat.net/sites/default/files/ confronting_csec_eng_0.pdf)

Thailand, Vietnam, Cambodia, the Philippines and Indonesia are only some of the other examples.

On 19 March 2015, ABC News reported:

> Paul Adhoch heads the UN agency Trace Kenya, which battles the trafficking of children. About 'sex tourists' he says: 'They are, specifically, deep in the communities, in poverty-stricken areas looking for sex – nothing else.' The port city of Mombasa has been a centre of trade (and formerly slavery) for hundreds of years and is now a hotspot for underage prostitution.
>
> Trace Kenya estimates there could be as many as 40,000 child sex workers in the city, and the trade extends up and down the seaside resort towns of Malindi and Diani. Mr Adhoch believes there is a community of paedophiles informing one another.

It would be a grave mistake to think that this problem is confined to Africa and Asia. The following example from Europe, if anything even more tragic, was featured in the London *Observer* newspaper on 31 January 2016, under the heading 'At least 10,000 refugee children "have vanished"':

> At least 10,000 unaccompanied child refugees have disappeared after arriving in Europe, according to the European Union's criminal intelligence agency. Many are feared to have fallen into the hands of organised trafficking syndicates.
>
> In the first attempt by law enforcement agencies to quantify one of the most worrying aspects of the migrant crisis, Europol's chief of staff told the *Observer* that thousands of vulnerable children had vanished after registering with state authorities.
>
> Brian Donald said 5,000 children had disappeared in Italy alone, while another 1,000 were unaccounted for in Sweden. He warned that a sophisticated pan-European 'criminal infrastructure' was now targeting refugees. 'It's not unreasonable to say that we're looking at 10,000-plus children. Not all of them will be criminally exploited; some might have been passed on to family members. We just don't know where they are, what they're doing or whom they are with.'...
>
> Donald confirmed Europol had received evidence that some unaccompanied child refugees in Europe had been sexually exploited... 'There are prisons in Germany and Hungary where the vast majority of people arrested and placed are in relation to criminal activity surrounding the migrant crisis.'
>
> The police agency has also documented a disturbing crossover between organised gangs helping to smuggle refugees into the EU and human-trafficking gangs exploiting them for sex work and slavery. He said that longstanding criminal gangs known to be involved in human trafficking were now being caught exploiting refugees.

To date we are told nothing about the connections between these gangs and those merchants of death who make fortunes out of trafficking migrants, thousands of whom have lost their lives at sea.

Then, on 12 April, 2016, the London *Times* reported:

> More than 5,000 migrant children have been reported missing in Germany amid the chaotic influx of 1.1 million people into the country.... Official figures showed that 5,835 children were reported missing last year in Germany, raising fears of abduction for sexual abuse or slavery... The missing, unaccompanied, underage children came mainly from Afghanistan, Syria, Eritrea, Morocco and Algeria...Of those officially listed as missing, 555 were younger than 14.

As a result of the war in Syria, originating in dictator Assad's suppression of opposition to his regime, one-fifth of neighbouring Jordan's population are Syrian refugees. The total of such refugees in the Middle East, and now in Europe, is more than four and a half million. They are living, women, men and children, in the most squalid and inhuman conditions in camps with barely habitable facilities and shelter.

At the other end of the world – after all do we not have 'globalisation'? – the same barbarism. Thirty-seven babies born on Australian soil have been sent to a remote atoll in the Pacific because their mothers are failed asylum seekers. More than 50 older children, 36 of them still at school, have been deported to Nauru, the world's smallest state, its area eight square miles.

Here we would do well to return to Marx's 'nothing to lose but their chains' and his earlier writing in *The Holy Family* of 1845: 'Absolutely imperative need – the practical expression of necessity – is what drives the proletariat to revolt against inhumanity.' And once again Germaine Greer:

> Female power will rush upon us in the persons of women who have nothing to lose, having lost everything already. It could

> surge up in China where so many women divorced for bearing girl children are living and working together, or in Thailand where prostitution and AIDS are destroying a generation, in Iran or anywhere else where women are on collision course with Islamic fundamentalism, or anywhere the famished labourer sees luxury foods for the western market grown on the land which used to provide for her and her children. And the women of the rich world had better hope that when female energy ignites they do not find themselves on the wrong side.
>
> (Greer, *The Whole Woman*, p.330.)

That last sentence is right. It has been argued by some feminists that these 'women of the rich world', with their access to facilities which can free them from much of the burden of childcare and confinement to the family home, are now in a position where they move towards equality, being able better to compete with men in the public sphere of jobs, politics, etc. But it goes without saying that it did not and does not apply in the slightest degree to the women of what was called the 'third world'. On the contrary, the families of many, many millions live in dire poverty and, in the recent period, are dispersed and terrorised by wars resulting from the attempts of the major capitalist powers to assert control of 'geopolitically' decisive areas and of the precious mineral resources of Africa, the Middle East and Asia. And in the 'advanced capitalist countries' of America and Western Europe, the relative advantages enjoyed by women and families are daily being eroded by the attacks on the welfare state and privatisation of public services, including child welfare and education, all consequent on the same structural crisis of capital which has led to the chaos in the Middle East. Those possibilities of health care, education, use of free time and so on are thus negated by the capital system's imperatives as its structural crisis unfolds. Since the onset of this crisis in the late 1960s and early 1970s the earlier reform concessions won by the working class have been under continuous attack, and the attack is being intensified.

This book focuses on the struggle to overcome the alienation inevitably forced upon us by the rule of capital, and above all with the role of women in that overcoming. In our twenty-first century, the inhumanity of the rule of capital, now 'globalised', takes the extreme form of humanitarian crises on an unprecedented scale. And this enhances greatly the role of women.

For politicians and financial journalists 'crisis' has become an over-used word. But in no case do they say, or understand, that today's crisis is not an occasional or conjunctural crisis like the 'boom and bust' and 'depression then recovery' of earlier days. There will still be such conjunctural crises, but they will come about as particular stages in what is now a permanent crisis. It is a structural, historical crisis of the capital system as a whole. It is the historical crisis of the last type of class society. That is to say, it is a historical crisis which will not end until the rule of capital comes to an end. Again, in our 'globalised' world it is manifested in a humanitarian crisis of global proportions. To address and set about resolving this crisis, there will have to be a consciousness, theoretical and practical, which contains not only the understanding that it is the rule of capital that must be ended and that the working class, capital's structural antagonist, is the only agency for that task. As we shall argue in Chapter 5, on class-consciousness, there must be a mass feeling of empathy with the sufferings of all the exploited and oppressed, and this is absolutely essential to the forging of the necessary solidarity. It is surely imperative that the human qualities necessary to achieve this must have at their heart those sensibilities which are particularly, even in some ways uniquely, characteristic of women; and first and foremost of those women who share the experience of the oppression and exploitation of the countless millions of women, and not only women, in the global population.

*Transition: from humanitarian crisis to class consciousness*

The propertied class and the class of the proletariat present the same self-estrangement. But the former class feels at ease and strengthened in this self-estrangement, it recognises estrangement as its own power and has in it the semblance of a human existence. The latter feels annihilated in estrangement; it sees in it its own powerlessness and the reality of an inhuman existence. It is, to use an expression of Hegel, in its abasement the indignation at that abasement, an indignation to which it is necessarily driven by the contradiction between its human nature and its condition of life, which is the outright, resolute and comprehensive negation of that nature…

When the proletariat is victorious, it by no means becomes the absolute side of society, for it is victorious only by abolishing itself and its opposite. Then the proletariat disappears as well as the opposite which determines it, private property.

When socialist writers ascribe this world-historic role to the proletariat, it is not at all…because they regard the proletarians as gods. Rather the contrary. Since in the fully-formed proletariat the abstraction of all humanity, even of the semblance of humanity, is practically complete; since the conditions of life of the proletariat sum up all the conditions of life of society today in their most inhuman form; since man has lost himself in the proletariat, yet at the same time has not only gained theoretical consciousness of that loss, but through urgent, no longer removable, no longer disguisable, absolutely imperative need – the practical expression of necessity – is driven directly to revolt against this inhumanity, it follows that the proletariat can and must emancipate itself. But it cannot emancipate itself without abolishing the conditions of its own life. It cannot abolish the conditions of its own life without abolishing all the inhuman conditions of life of society today which are summarised in its own situation. Not in vain does it go through the stern but steeling school of labour. It is not a question of what this or that proletarian, or even the whole proletariat, at the moment regards as its aim. It is a question of what the proletariat

> is, and what, in accordance with this being, it will historically be compelled to do.
>
> (Marx and Engels, *The Holy Family*, in *MECW, vol. 4,* 1844-45, pp.36-7)

Because we are concentrating on the relation between our global human crisis, class-consciousness, and the condition and role of women, this passage has here a particular importance. Unlike almost all discussions of class consciousness it does not treat only of the material, i.e., economic and political position of the working class. Marx and Engels write here of the being of the proletariat in its condition of alienation, estrangement, of the inhumanity to which it is subjected. Our next chapter takes up the question of class-consciousness on that basis.

CHAPTER 5

# 'CLASS-CONSCIOUSNESS' AND WOMEN

We have seen (following Marx), that the oppression and exploitation of working people are destructive of their whole 'being', amounting to deprivation of their humanity: Marx writes of 'their spiritual and physical misery' (*Contribution to the Critique of Hegel's Philosophy of Law*, in *MECW*, vol. 4, pp.175-6), and thus not merely an economic and political oppression. There are obvious implications for the socialist class-consciousness necessary for the social revolution.

In considering these implications, it follows that it must be borne in mind that class-consciousness will have to be a matter not only of reasoned understanding of the necessity of social revolution, but must be a practical consciousness, i.e., must be expressed in organisation and action (see Cliff Slaughter, *Bonfire of the Certainties*, Lulu, 2013). For example, in terms of the issues raised by today's manifestations of our human crisis, organisation and action which help to sustain communities, countering the deliberate scattering of families in wars as a weapon of dispersing and aiming to make impossible working people's resistance, is practical class-consciousness, without which a transition from defensive to offensive action against the enemy would be impossible. In that fight the role of women is crucial.

But we must go further. If class-consciousness means that the whole 'being' of the working class is to be understood and changed, then we must not restrict our understanding to economic and political consciousness. This 'being' surely refers to the whole man, and the whole woman, their alienation, amounting to a 'dehumanisation', and this surely does not mean only their material conditions. And from this it follows that class-consciousness, in theory and in practice, requires not only rational understanding. It can be complete and effective only when vitally infused with solidarity, which is impossible without emotion, passion, empathy, anger, feeling, fellow-feeling and indignation, and hope.

Class-consciousness understood in this way, manifested in the class struggle for a new society, was already at the core of the work of the young Marx. In 1843 he showed how it is essential to go beyond the criticism of religion and 'criticise' in theory and in practice the condition of life which gives rise to religion: 'Religion is the sigh of the oppressed creature, the heart of a heartless world, just as it is the spirit of unspiritual conditions. It is the opium of the people.' And: 'The criticism of religion ends with the teaching that man is the highest being for man, hence with the categorical imperative to overthrow all relations in which man is a debased, enslaved, forsaken, despicable being.' (*MECW*, vol. 3, p.182.)

Here we have the humanism which is central to Marx's whole outlook, and so invisible to those critics who see him as an 'economic determinist'. As Ernst Bloch expressed it: 'This impassioned man feels that he is himself a human being and ... others are human beings too and yet for the most part are treated like dogs.' (Ernst Bloch, *The Principle of Hope*, MIT Press, 1995, vol. 3, p.1357.) For Bloch, hope is 'the most important' of the 'expectant emotions' – those 'like anxiety, fear, hope, belief' which are distinguished by their particular 'anticipatory character' – and it is 'the most human of all mental feelings': it reaches for 'the furthest and brightest horizon', the horizon of the future society of free and equal individuals. (Bloch, *op. cit.*, vol. 1, pp.74-5.) It is worth remembering too that Hegel, who, despite his closed system limited to the past and the present, could write in his *Phenomenology*, 'Nothing great has ever been achieved without passion'.

Antonio Gramsci knew that for there to be a 'favourable situation' for revolution there must be fighting ardour in the working class. (Quintin Hoare and Geoffrey Nowell Smith, eds., *Selections From the Prison Notebooks of Antonio Gramsci*, Lawrence and Wishart, 1971, pp.177-85). And for Rosa Luxemburg this element of revolutionary will could only come about in real-life struggle:

> ...for the first time in history, the popular masses themselves, in opposition to the ruling classes, are to impose their will but they must first effect this outside of the present society, beyond the existing society. This will the masses can only form in a constant struggle against the existing order. The union of the broad popular masses with an aim reaching beyond the existing social order, the union of the daily struggle with the great world transformation, that is the task of the Social-Democratic [read 'socialist', CS] movement, which must logically grope on its road of development between the following two rocks: abandoning the mass character of the party or, abandoning its final aim, falling into bourgeois reformism or into sectarianism, anarchism or opportunism.
>
> (See chapter 10 of Rosa Luxemburg's *Reform or Revolution, 2nd edition,* 1908.)

Marx has very often been understood as an 'economic determinist'. In reality, the emphasis we have laid here on the element of will and emotion and on the nature of consciousness as practical consciousness is central to Marx's basic outlook. This is absolutely specific in his *Theses onFeuerbach*, where he criticises materialists who failed to grasp reality as 'human sensuous activity, practice (praxis)'. Only from this standpoint could communism be understood: 'The abolition of private property is therefore the complete emancipation of all human senses and qualities, but it is this emancipation precisely because these senses and attributes have become, subjectively and objectively, human.' Incidentally, if some would-be hard-headed revolutionists like to cite Lenin as their predecessor and inspiration, they should go back not only to his last testament (1924), the impassioned denunciation of Stalin's rudeness and bullying, and to a passage in his *What is to be Done*, rarely quoted:

> 'We should dream'! I wrote these words and became alarmed. I imagined myself sitting at a 'unity conference' and opposite me were the *RabocheyeDyelo* editors and contributors. Comrade Martynov rises and, turning to me, says sternly: 'Permit me to ask you, has an autonomous editorial board the right to dream without first soliciting the opinion of the Party committees?' He is followed by Comrade Krichevsky, who (philosophically deepening Comrade Martynov, who long ago rendered Comrade Plekhanov more profound) continues even more sternly: 'I go further. I ask, has a Marxist any right at all to dream, knowing that according to Marx mankind always sets itself the tasks its can solve and that tactics is a process of the growth of Party tasks which grow together with the Party?'
>
> The very thought of these stern questions sends a cold shudder down my spine and makes me wish for nothing but a place to hide in. I shall try to hide behind the back of Pisarev.
>
> 'There are rifts and rifts,' wrote Pisarev of the rift between dreams and reality. 'My dream may run ahead of the natural march of events or may fly off at a tangent in a direction in which no natural march of events will ever proceed. In the first case my dream will not cause any harm; it may even support and augment the energy of the working men... There is nothing in such dreams that would distort or paralyse labour-power. On the contrary, if man were completely deprived of the ability to dream in this way, if he could not from time to time run ahead and mentally conceive, in an entire and completed picture, the product to which his hands are only just beginning to lend shape, then I cannot at all imagine what stimulus there would be to induce man to undertake and complete extensive and strenuous work in the sphere of art, science, and practical endeavour... The rift between dreams and reality causes no harm if only the person dreaming believes seriously in his dreams, if he attentively observes life, compares his

> observations with his castles in the air, and if, generally speaking, he works conscientiously for the achievement of his fantasies. If there is some connection between dreams and life then all is well.'
>
> Of this kind of dreaming there is unfortunately too little in our movement. And the people most responsible for this are those who boast of their sober views, their 'closeness' to the 'concrete'...
>
> (Lenin, *Collected Works, vol.* 5, Progress Publishers, 1960, pp.509-10)

When socialists have tried to build 'vanguard' revolutionary parties to 'bring revolutionary consciousness to the working class from the outside', they have seen that consciousness only in economic (material) and political terms (a mistake in addition to the notion of 'from the outside'). For this reason, as we shall see in a later chapter, such would-be revolutionary parties have often been reduced to a sect or cult existence, replicating the inhuman moral order of the society they set out to overthrow. On such a basis in theory as in practice, there is no possibility of what is an indispensable element in the working class's long and arduous road to a new social order, namely, that the preparation, in ideas and in practice, for transition to that future order must develop and contain the anticipation of the future free and equal relation between human beings, men and women.

The understanding of 'imperative need' as the immediate spur to revolution surely cannot be understood unless we are fully aware of the emotional and passionate content of class-consciousness. It is not surprising that great writers such as Stendhal, Albert Camus and Vasily Grossman saw this side of the matter. In *Life and Fate*, Grossman's masterpiece published in 1960, we find, amid all the cruelty and misery of war, inspiring examples of human sympathy and generosity of spirit. Stendhal, in his *Life of Henri Brulard* (Penguin Classics, 1973, p.34), writes: 'I have always, as it were by some instinct, despised the bourgeoisie... So then, according to me, energy was only to be found, in my opinion [this was in 1811], in that class which has to struggle with real needs.' And Camus in *The First Man* – his final, unfinished novel (not published till 1994, 44 years after his death in a car accident) – gives us a compelling picture of the warmth and sympathy so important in the fight to live through and overcome hardship. He writes: 'For me honour in the world is found among the oppressed, not those who hold power. And it is from that [power] alone that dishonour arises.' (Albert Camus, *The First Man*, Penguin, 1996, p.230). It is interesting here to recall the way in which 'left' writers such as Sartre, de Beauvoir and Merleau-Ponty shunned and denounced Camus. They were 'fellow-travellers' of the Stalinist Communist Party of France, and as late as the 1960s, long after Khrushchev's revelations of Stalin's crimes and the brutal suppression of the Hungarian Revolution in 1956, they remained at the level of 'hands off the Soviet Union!' and refused to countenance any criticism of the Soviet regime. And so Camus's refusal to remain silent about the inhumanity of the Stalinist purges and atrocities was seen by them as a capitulation to the bourgeoisie.

If we take together 'nothing to lose but their chains', the inferior status and imprisonment of women in the modern family, the hitherto grossly neglected element of feeling and emotion in class-consciousness, the magnitude and depth of our global humanitarian crisis manifested in war- and mass starvation and especially its impact on women and children, do women have an 'interest' in the struggle for and achievement of social revolution? We maintain that they do. And the recognition of that 'interest' is the germ of women's class-consciousness – the class-consciousness of the working class against capital, and not, of course, the class of women against men. This same recognition is the germ of a great development in the consciousness (theoretical and practical, we repeat) of working men, and thus, of the class. The absolutely necessary struggle of women against their oppression and exploitation is central to overcoming the rule of capital, and in the fight for a truly human society (our second human revolution), men too will have to learn this. Again the young Marx, this time a year later, in the *Economic and Philosophical Manuscripts of 1844* insists – in a way directly relevant to our argument in this book:

> In the approach to *woman* as the *spoil* and handmaid of communal lust is expressed the infinite degradation in which man exists for himself, for the secret of this approach has its unambiguous, decisive, plain and undisguised expression in the relation of man to woman and in the manner in which the direct and natural species-relationship is conceived. The direct, natural and necessary relation of person to person is the *relation of man to woman*. In this natural species-relationship man's relation to nature is immediately his relation to man, just as his relation to man is immediately his relation to nature – his own natural destination. In this relationship, therefore, is *sensuously manifested*, reduced to an observable *fact*, the extent to which the human essence has become nature to man, or to which nature to him has become the human essence of man. From this relationship one can therefore judge man's whole level of development. From the character of this relationship follows how much *man* as a *species-being*, as man, has come to be himself and to comprehend himself; the relation of man to woman is the *most natural* relation of human being to human being. It therefore reveals the extent to which man's *natural* behaviour has become *human*, or the extent to which the *human* essence in him has become a *natural* essence – the extent to which his human *nature* has come to be *natural* to him. This relationship also reveals the extent to which man's *need* has become a *human* need; the extent to which, therefore, the *other* person as a person, as a person has become for him a need – the extent to which he in his individual existence is at the same time a social being.
>
> (*MECW, vol. 3*, pp.295-6.)

We are at a stage, because of the depth of the global crisis, where, as argued in our introduction, the indispensable role of women in the struggle of the working class takes on a greater importance than ever, because of women's superior sensibility to the sufferings of others. We may recall John Berger's essay on Frida Kahlo and her art:

> That she became a world legend is in part due to the fact that in the dark age in which we are living under the new world order,

> the sharing of pain is one of the essential preconditions for a refounding of dignity and hope. Much pain is unbearable. But the will to share pain is shareable. And from that inevitably inadequate sharing comes a resistance.
>
> (John Berger, *The Shape of a Pocket,* Bloomsbury, 2002, p.164.)

To summarise the argument thus far. The revolution of the working class for socialism is best understood as the (second) human revolution. The achievements of the first human revolution were negated by the birth of private property in the means of production, class society, the state and the patriarchal monogamous family. The latter was 'the world-historical defeat of the female sex'. When that 'negation' is negated by the social revolution, the oppression of women will be negated. Hence the vital interest of women in that revolution, so that in that way their struggle and their true liberation coincides with the struggle and liberation of men.

The structural crisis of the capital system is today manifested in an unprecedented humanitarian crisis, and for the empathy, understanding and solidarity needed to confront that crisis the particular sensibilities of women make their role, as one half of the proletariat, more vital than ever. In order to grasp the depth and the proportions of this role, we need to grasp a hitherto neglected aspect of class-consciousness, i.e., the importance of feeling and passion in that consciousness.

CHAPTER 6

# A MOUNTAIN TO CLIMB

## CAN WE OVERCOME THE SORRY RECORD OF THE TREATMENT OF WOMEN IN 'REVOLUTIONARY' MOVEMENTS AND SELF-STYLED 'SOCIALIST' REGIMES?

In 1991 Cliff Slaughter and the social anthropologist Frank Girling visited Namibia to meet dissident liberation activists, amongst whom were twin sisters Panduleni and Ndamona Kali. They had an until-then little-heard story to tell, and Slaughter and Girling arranged for them to come to the UK to tell it. When Panduleni died 19 years later, Paul Trewhela, the anti-Stalinist fighter against apartheid – who, having edited the underground freedom journal *Umkhonto we Sizwe* at the time of the Rivonia trial, broken with the South African Communist Party while a political prisoner in the mid-1960s and gone on to publish the revelatory *Inside Quatro: Uncovering the Exile History of the ANC and Swapo* (Jacana Media, 2009) – wrote that she 'was an outstanding and emblematic woman of contemporary southern Africa [whose] life embodied the schizophrenic contradictions of the region, torn between suffering and modernity.' (See *The Independent*, London, 10 September 2010.) The twins' story is also of central relevance to the theme of this book and of significance far beyond its southern African context.

Panduleni, when she died, had risen in the Namibian government service to be Deputy Director in the Ministry of Labour; but, stressed Trewhela, what was remarkable about 'her distinguished professional' career was that it had 'taken shape after a terrible experience when she and Ndamona, were in their 20s.'

> For almost six years in the 1980s, the twin sisters and well over a hundred other Namibian women endured torture and imprisonment in pits in southern Angola at the hands of men who led the organisation to which they had dedicated their youthful political energies, the South West Africa People's Organisation (SWAPO). Since 1990 SWAPO has been the sole governing party of Namibia; over the previous 24 years it had been engaged in a guerrilla war against white South African rule.

Born in 1958, the sisters had become involved in political activity in the Namibian Black Students' Organisation when they were at school in Omaruru, north of Windhoek. Harassed by the South African police, they left the country for Angola for military training with SWAPO's People's Liberation Army of Namibia (PLAN). Ndamona was then sent to the Komsomol (the Communist Party of the Soviet Union youth organisation) in Moscow for political training, Panduleni to Cuba – to the Federation of Cuban Women. After completing her course, Ndamona returned to SWAPO in Angola before being sent to join Panduleni at Cuba's University of Camaguey, where they studied economics. Both were leaders, Ndamonaof the SWAPO youth at the university, Panduleniof the women's council.

Let Ndamona, who has contributed the following account for this book, take up the story.

> We [had] joined the political organisation at the tender age of 15 and were SWAPO activists inside the country while still attending our secondary education at Martin Luther High School. Due to political pressure and the imminent arrest by the South African regime we were forced to leave the country and join SWAPO in Angola.
>
> After completing military training we were sent to the then Soviet Union and Cuba respectively for political training. [I] later joined Pandu in Cuba to enter … university, [intending] to graduate in

the field of Planning of National Economy … But this was not to be as our studies were abruptly cut short.

On the instruction of SWAPO we were forcefully removed from the university premises to the point that our belongings were packed by the Cuban Security in our absence and in full view of other students (national and international). After being internally searched by one of the female Security Officers we were further humiliated by being handcuffed and escorted from one of the rooms we were kept in to the car that transported us from Camaguey to Havana – a journey that took us more than eight hours. We … were kept in prison for a week. Upon our insistence – accompanied by a refusal to eat – we managed to secure a visit by a gentleman, completely unknown to us, … who told us that we were needed by SWAPO. When the gentleman reappeared in the plane it later was clear that he was a SWAPO security man, whose mission was to take us to SWAPO dungeons in Lubango, the 'Karl Marx Reception Centre' in southern Angola.

Our journey to the airport in Havana was nothing short of a drama. We were escorted to the military airport by security officers in the car, and … armed vehicles – two in the front and two in the rear, while one was ahead clearing the way… An ambulance was also part of the convoy. Then, when we arrived at the airport in Angola we were locked up in a warehouse-like room by the Cuban military staff until the SWAPO people arrived and we were put into a truck that was completely sealed, … were not aware in which direction we were being driven and … were told not to ask any questions.

After a couple of days travel, we arrived at the first camp, called the screening camp, where interrogation and torturing started. The questions were three: 'When, where and by whom were you recruited to work for the enemy?'

We were separated, and for more than two years we did not know about one another's whereabouts and whether one of us had succumbed to the tortures or not.The tortures were meant to extract a false confession because the more you told the truth, the more the tortures were exerted. The torture chambers were mostly used in the nights and those doing the beatings with sticks were mostly men. We were asked to undress and the beatings were done on the bare skin.

The methods of torture we endured were (1) being blindfolded with hands bound behind the back, cloth in the mouth and told to sit flat on the ground while different men start with the beating while repeating the three questions; (2) having the hands tied at one end of a horizontal pole and the legs on the other end, facing down, so that the blood-flow to the head was immense and there was excruciating pain from the beatings ... causing fainting every time they used the method; (3) with two thick sticks ... tied at one end together ... being told to insert your head between the sticks and while the head is between the sticks the other end is firmly tied, and the more their questions are not responded to their satisfaction, the tighter they do it; (4) having a finger ... put in a knot of a thread, usually of an animal vein, tied on one end of a bowed stick, with the other end ... tied on the other end of the stick and made tighter and tighter for the period of the interrogation, so that the thread around the finger gets deeper and deeper causing an immense pain beyond any measure.

After months and months of solitary confinement and torture they succeeded in exacting false confessions which unfortunately tainted our names forever.

UN Security Council Resolution 435 adopted as long before as September 1978 making proposals for a cease-fire and UN-supervised elections in South African-controlled South West Africa which ultimately led to the independence of Namibia was finally implemented and we – together with the rest of the SWAPO prisoners – arrived home in 1989 under a cloud of mistrust and hatred from those who labelled us spies. Calls to SWAPO to clear our names or put us through a competent court of law to defend and clear our names fell on deaf ears.

After two years of unemployment we landed clerical jobs in the

> Government in the Statistics Office: our potential was noted by the Director of the Statistics Office, who was a UN employee tasked to set up the country office and we were awarded scholarships by the UN to further our studies.The decision did not go unchallenged by those who believed that 'spies' were not worthy of the opportunity but thanks to the steadfastness of the Director, it came to pass. After three years we completed the Bachelor of Statistics (Hons) making us the first Namibians to graduate as statisticians.

Trewhela's account adds details supplied by Panduleni. The twins' Angolan prison, in which they were kept for five years, consisted of 'damp pits in the ground', he wrote: '"There was a small layer of bricks at the top of the hole to serve as windows", Panduleni told me.'

> We covered ourselves with empty rice bags, sleeping on boxes [she said]. In one corner there was the toilet, and we were so overcrowded that the last person had to sleep only a few centimetres from the toilet. There was no fresh air. The dug-out served as hospital, dining room, toilet, and even in one case as maternity room.

Twice the women were visited by the SWAPO leader, and subsequent president of Namibia, Sam Nujoma, who, though told the allegations against them were false and shown the marks of the beatings, took no action. On the contrary, Panduleni told Trewhela:

> Nujoma said that we were enemy agents, that we came with poisons to kill the combatants of PLAN, some of us even tested our poisons, we put them in the water and food of PLAN combatants, and these people died. He promised that they would fight more than ever to liberate Namibia, and to take us to our mothers and fathers, and we would be paraded at a revolutionary square where they were going to hoist their flag and the nation would decide what to do with us.'

Having made a successful transition from prisoner to senior government official, Panduleni, in June 1999, accompanied the then Minister of Labour, Andimba Toivoya Toivo – a founder of SWAPO, long-term prisoner on Robben Island, and a revered Namibian political leader – to a conference of the International Labour Organisation in Geneva. Ten years earlier the sisters had been forced to make 'confessions' on video, and it had been the same Toivo who had presented them to journalists from Germany, France, Angola, Cuba and Namibia, as 'traitors who had betrayed their nation', but who had been forgiven and were going to be returned to Namibia.

*

There can be few more compelling examples of the entirely negative and often disastrous component of the outlook of would-be socialist revolutionists expressed by the old adage, 'The end justifies the means'.

Instead, the means used by those working for human progress must be consistent with the ends. That is the only foundation for a socialist morality. This is not a mere abstract principle. In the many-sided movement working for the change to socialism, to the human revolution, human beings must surely treat each other with humanity. Sadly, that has by no means always been the case, and that is a massive understatement. In what follows there are several examples. These examples would not have occurred if there had been any understanding, in theory and in practice, of what we have shown to be the essential role of women in the working-class movement. Here 'in practice' means that the living experience of the working-class movement must build an anticipation, a hope and a foretaste of that future society of free and equal individuals which is our objective. This is what Germaine Greer was driving at when she wrote, in *The Female Eunuch*, these inspired words: 'The surest guide to the correctness of the path that women take is joy in the struggle. Revolution is the festival of the oppressed.' (Greer, *The Female Eunuch*, p.330.)

It has to be said that, with some honourable exceptions, the working-class movement, dominated by men in organisations from trade unions to would-be revolutionary parties and then to states claiming to be socialist, has neglected the conditions and the role of women. Worse than that, class society's infliction of an inferior status upon women has been replicated. Worse still, there has been gross abuse of women by men who held positions of power in their organisations.

In 1936 Trotsky wrote, under the heading 'Thermidor in the Family',

> The [Russian] revolution made a heroic effort to destroy the so-called family hearth – that archaic, stuffy, and stagnant institution in which the woman of the toiling classes performs galley labour from childhood to death. The place of the family as a shut-in petty enterprise was to be occupied, according to the plans, by a finished system of social care and accommodation: maternity houses, child-care centres, kindergartens, schools, social dining rooms, social laundries, first-aid stations, hospitals, sanatoria, athletic organisations, moving-picture theatres, etc. The complete absorption of the housekeeping functions of the family by institutions of the socialist society, uniting all generations in solidarity and mutual aid, was to bring to woman, and thereby to the loving couple, a real liberation from the thousand-year-old fetters.... The actual liberation of women is unrealisable on a basis of generalised want.
>
> (L D Trotsky, *The Revolution Betrayed*, New Park, 1976, chap.5)

By the time *The Revolution Betrayed* was written, Stalin and his apparatus had imposed the repressive regime of 'socialism in one country' in economically backward Russia, in defiance of the above truth about 'generalised want'. This meant a whole system of counter-revolutionary actions and measures: the Moscow show trials which sentenced and executed every possible rival to Stalin and every survivor of the old Bolshevik leadership; forced collectivisation of the peasantry involving mass murder and mass impoverishment and starvation; forced labour in prison camps. It meant also the reinforcement of women's oppression. One of Stalin's appointees, Aaron Soltz, a 'specialist on matrimonial matters', declared on the forthcoming prohibition of abortion that in a socialist society there are so many good things such as 'no unemployment', so that 'a woman has no right to refuse the joys of motherhood.' Trotsky commented, 'The philosophy of a priest endowed with the powers of a gendarme.'

And so the age-old oppression and exploitation of ordinary women continued, and was intensified by the totalitarian terror regime of the Stalinist state. As ever, for the ladies of top brass things were very different. Simon Sebag Montefiore tells us:

> The Politburo ladies now had heir own haute couture designer. All the 'top ten families' went to the atelier on KatuzovskyProspekt, controlled by an MGB department, where Abram ...Lerner and Nina Adzhubei designed the men's suits and the women's dresses...
>
> Once the grandees of Victorian Europe had taken the waters at the Bohemian resort of Carlsbad. Now ZinaidaZhdanova and Nina Beria held court here. 'Lavishly dressed and covered in furs', with her daughter in a 'mink stole', Polina[Molotova] often arrived at the same spa in an official plane with an entourage of fifty. Her daughter Svetlana, a real 'Bolshevik princess', was chauffeured daily to the Institute of Foreign Relations, where many of the elite studied, 'arriving in a cloud of Chanel No.5, wearing a new outfit every day'...
>
> [Stalin] consoled the family of Shcherbakov, the Moscow boss who died of alcoholism, with a shower of cash. Stalin specified: 'Give them an apartment with a dacha, rights to the Kremlin hospital, limousine... NKVD special staff ... teacher for children...' He awarded Shcherbakov's widow 2,000 roubles a month, his sons 1,000 a month until graduation, his mother 700 a month, his sister 300. His wife also received a lump sum of 200,000 roubles and his mother 50,000 roubles – sums of unthinkable munificence for the average worker. Here was Stalin's new imperial order.
>
> (Simon Sebag Montefiore, *The Court of the Red Tsar*, Weidenfeld and Nicholson paperback, 2003, pp.565-6)

This was the 'classless society' according to the doctrine and the reality of 'socialism in one country'.

> Stalin carefully targeted the families of 'enemies'. "'They had to be isolated,' explained Molotov, 'otherwise they'd have spread all kinds of complaints…'"
>
> On 5 July 1937, the Politburo ordered the NKVD to 'confine all wives of condemned traitors in camps for five to eight years' and to take under state protection children under fifteen: 18,000 wives and 25,000 children were taken away. But this was not enough: on 15 August Yezhov declared that children between one and three be confined in orphanages but 'socially dangerous' children between three and fifteen could be imprisoned 'depending on the degree of danger'. Almost a million of these children were raised in orphanages and often did not see their mothers for twenty years.
>
> (Montefiore, *op. cit.*, p.237.)

Some of these mothers were among the thousands murdered by the state agencies.

Stalin himself shows us best how the old attitudes persisted, one might say were perfected, under 'socialism in one country'. Just before the 'Big Three' summit meeting at Yalta with Roosevelt and Churchill in July 1944, 'the Second and Third Byelorussian Fronts broke into East Prussia, Germany itself, in a fiesta of vengeance':

> two million German women were to be raped in the coming months. Russian soldiers even raped Russian women newly liberated from Nazi camps. Stalin cared little about this, telling the Yugoslav writer Milovan Djilas: 'You have of course read Dostoievsky? Do you see what a complicated thing is man's soul …? Well then, imagine a man who has fought from Stalingrad to Belgrade – over thousands of kilometres of his own devastated land, across the dead bodies of his comrades and dearest ones? How can such a man react normally? And what is so awful about his having fun with a woman after such horror?'
>
> (Montefiore, *op.cit.*, p.489.)

In the 'People's Republic' of China, there are many similar stories. There, the position and role of women was treated in a way reminiscent of the population control advocated long ago by Malthus and resorted to by reactionary ideologists and regimes in 'the West' ever since. First Mao had told women to 'have as many children as possible.' Then, in the late 1970s, there had to be only one child per family, the bureaucracy's 'experts' having calculated that the ideal size of population for China was 700 million. A year-by-year timetable was worked out to achieve this noble goal. Then in 2015 the policy changed: you can have two children (Mei Fong, *One Child: The Story of China's Most Radical Experiment,* 2016). A reviewer in the London *Observer* described Mei Fong's book as 'a harrowing account of the decisions of a small coterie of men with too much faith in science and ideology and too little in humanity.' Now, despite the Chinese 'communist' leaders' professed belief that 'woman's place is in the home', we find that there are 20 million children living in villages without their mothers, who have been forced to work in the urban centres.

We have seen how women played their part in the struggle for an independent Ireland. But that independence, when achieved, hardly brought about a liberation of women. Ironically, if that is the right word, Margaret Skinnider, who had been wounded during the Easter Rising, was refused a pension in the days of De Valera's government on the grounds that the relevant law was 'applicable to soldiers as generally understood in the masculine sense'(!). The Army finance officer wrote saying he had sought legal advice and that the definition of 'wound' in the Act 'only contemplated the masculine gender' and that the reference to 'any person' was 'referable only to the male sex' (contemplated??, a woman is not 'a person'??). This action and the justification offered for it were a direct reflection of the Irish regime after the country became independent.

The leaders of the 1916 rebellion, Padraig Pearse and James Connolly, who had declared and upheld the principles of women's equality and their role in the struggle in their Easter address to 'Irish Men and Irish Women', had been executed by the British establishment. Many of the rebels were imprisoned and some executed. In the next two years the

Roman Catholic Church, whose leaders had condemned the Rising, very deliberately moved to put itself in a position to head off the mass feeling aroused by Britain's brutal repression, and declared for the revolutionaries. But the reactionary ideology of the Church was fully reasserted in the Irish Free State, established in 1922-3, and then the Republic. Irish leaders like Eamonn De Valera, who had nothing whatsoever in common with Pearse and Connolly, were dominated by the Church. De Valera's constitution of 1937 outlawed contraception and divorce was banned. Article 41 of the constitution defined the duty of the state to 'endeavour to ensure that mothers shall not be obliged to engage in labour to the neglect of their duties in the home.' In the Republic, abortion was illegal ('unless it occurs as the result of a medical intervention performed to save the life of the mother'). It is regulated by the Protection of Life During Pregnancy Act 2013.

Olivia O'Leary wrote about the position of women in Ireland in *The Guardian* of 25 March 2016:

> Women public servants – doctors, nurses, teachers, television producers – had to resign because of their positions on marriage. They might be re-employed in a temporary capacity but at a reduced salary. There were always lower rates of pay for women in the public and the private sector. This continued right up into the 70s, and a male-dominated establishment – including the trade union movement – went along with it.

Similarly, in the revolutionary struggles in Cuba and in dozens of national liberation struggles, the women who fought were soon to be reminded in no uncertain terms that, as before, 'woman's place is in the home'.

Revolutions were successful in overthrowing the capitalist state in Russia and China, but they remained internationally isolated, and so the social conditions they achieved were limited to those of a backward economy and culture. In these conditions of 'generalised want' the bureaucratic utopia of 'socialism in a single country' inevitably meant that the liberation of women, essential part of the transition to socialism, was unattainable.

But what can be said, in terms of 'the objective conditions', of those organisations in the labour and socialist movement where backward, reactionary attitudes and conduct towards women have prevailed? In the trade unions, despite the many, many heroic struggles for equal pay, for better working conditions and for workers' rights, women have been almost completely excluded from leadership positions, and that exclusion continues to this day. Women are only a small minority of the parliamentary representatives of the reformist and 'labour' parties.

In the last few decades, one 'revolutionary' party ('sect' would be a more accurate designation) after another has been exposed and has imploded after their members escaped from or rose up against their leaders' systematic sexual abuse of women and girls. Only recently, one Aravindan Balakrishnan was handed a sentence of two years in prison for his abuse of women and girls in his south London 'Workers' Institute of Marxism-Leninism – Mao Zedong Thought'. Victims told *The Times* that this outfit, in what amounted to a fortress-house in Brixton, was intended to be 'a pilot unit where Balakrishnan could learn how to control people before he could take over the world.' Balakrishnan's daughter, like others, was confined to the house, suffering his iron control and brutality. She escaped in her teens, only to be brought back. On her return '…the violence escalated and her father branded her as a fascist agent.'

This is easily recognised as an extreme case, a cult with its guru, of which there are many examples without any pretensions to 'Marxism-Leninism' and the like. The personal power syndrome, the delusions of grandeur, and the obsession with control and 'security' are common to them all. All the same, it must be recognised that the Balakrishnan cult, claiming to be revolutionary, was only one of the sects on the left making the same claim and ending up with the same kind of internal degeneration.

In Britain the Workers Revolutionary Party (WRP), led until 1985 by Gerry Healy, was surely the most notorious of the sects. There is no doubt that this 'party' was held together by the devotion of its members to what they saw as the need for socialist revolution and the truth of the theories of Marx, in this case as developed by Trotsky and his fight against Stalinism, and not by some faith in the mission of a self-proclaimed saviour. But they found themselves confronted, in 1985, by the revelations made by a small group of comrades working at the party centre who, acting courageously in the circumstances, produced irrefutable proof that Healy, the WRP's general secretary, had for years systematically sexually abused women members. Healy was summarily expelled. The findings of the party's Control Commission on this abuse are detailed in the published account by one of its members, Norman Harding (*Staying Red: Why I am still a Socialist*. See https://staying red.wordpress.com). More recently, in 2013, the Socialist Workers' Party in Britain was heavily damaged when many resigned in protest at how allegations against a leading member that he had raped a female comrade had been dealt with.

Over decades in the Workers' Revolutionary Party and its predecessor the Socialist Labour League, Healy's ideas and his morality had degenerated. He had become prominent as a young worker in the Trotskyist movement in the years just preceding the Second World War. In the post-war years he became more and more obsessed with the notion of building a party of 'professional revolutionaries' – actually a corps of area organisers charged with recruitment of members and collection of funds, together with journalists, print-workers and office workers at the party centre, all full-time paid employees, who were effectively cut off from the real life of the working class by exaggerated concerns with 'security', tightly controlled and most of them confined to the party centre. This was no more than a mechanical adaptation of Lenin's idea of building a party in the particular conditions of illegality under Tsarist rule. It was an organisational form which turned out to be perfectly designed for Healy's depraved sexual pursuits. Here was an effective screen permitting Healy, now sure that he was the genuine article, Trotsky's successor as the leader of the Fourth International, to tell his victims that succumbing to his sexual demands was essential for their 'training'. By the 1970s Healy had convinced himself that he was a leading theoretician and expert in Marxist 'philosophy', lecturing and writing on dialectics and Hegel. What he produced was mumbo-jumbo.

These examples are of interest here only because in them we see that the patriarchal oppression and prejudice at the core of class society persist stubbornly, and can even take obscene forms, even when the perpetrators avow revolutionary convictions, sometimes sincerely. They tell us that what is necessary is the fight for a truly human understanding of the alienation imposed by the rule of capital. Such a human understanding and the practice which it informs must have at their centre the realisation that the capital system and its state depend unconditionally on the oppression of women, and the conviction that the role of women in the fight for socialism is equal to and an absolutely necessary complement to that of men. It cannot be repeated too often that we must go beyond the hope and belief that a future socialist order of society will bring the liberation of women. The forms of struggle and organisation for the social revolution must actually anticipate and begin to build the lineaments of that liberated state to which socialists aspire: the community of free and equal individuals.

CHAPTER 7

# WHAT DOES ANTHROPOLOGY TELL US?

Over the last hundred years, anthropologists have been able to study and describe many, many more of the world's peoples still depending on hunting and gathering and elementary horticulture and herding than were previously known. A small number of these tribal societies have survived because they remained isolated until very recently, but in almost all cases they have been subjected to colonisation (and some, as in the case of the Aborigines of Australia, decimated), so that it is not easy to know to what degree the traditional social forms and culture have changed. In the Appendix, Steve Drury writes on the relevance of the mores of surviving hunter-gatherer societies to those before the Neolithic, about which we can only surmise from slim evidence. For one thing, then all parts of every ecosystem were available to them.

And so, to the questions, 'Does anthropology show us that in classless, stateless societies, without private property in the means of production, women were more equal than they became after the beginning of class-divided societies?', 'Was group marriage or promiscuity ever the rule?' and 'Were no "primitive" societies monogamous?' there is no definite answer covering all or most examples.

Here we cannot do better than to summarise and quote from the work of outstanding anthropologist Kathleen Gough. She spent her life examining this question, from every angle. Her conclusions were summarised in the essay 'The Origin of the Family' (a deliberate take on Engels' classic *Origin of the Family, Private Property and the State* published in a volume edited by Rayna R. Reiter, *Towards an Anthropology of Women* (Monthly Review Press, 1975, pp.54-76). The following passages are taken from that essay.

> [There] are arrangements where there is sexual access to members of a kin group (e.g., Eskimos and some other hunters). Similarly, many hunting societies hold that wives of brothers or other close kinsmen are in some senses wives of the group. They can be called on in emergencies or if one of them is ill. Again, many hunting societies have special times for sexual licence between men and women who are not married to each other. (Op. cit., p.68.)
>
> In general in hunting societies... women are less subordinated in certain crucial respects than they are in most, if not all, of the archaic states, or even in some capitalist nations... Especially lacking in hunting societies is the kind of male possessiveness and exclusiveness regarding women that leads to such institutions as savage punishments or death for female adultery, the jealous guarding of female chastity and virginity, the denial of divorce to women, or the ban on a woman's remarriage after her husband's death...There is reciprocity rather than domination or exploitation.
>
> As Engels saw, the power of men to exploit women systematically springs from the existence of surplus wealth, and more directly from the state, social stratification, and the control of property by men. (Op. cit., pp.69-70.)
>
> With horticulture society is more likely to be or to remain matrilocal and to develop matrilineal descent groups with a relatively high status of women. (Op. cit., p.73.)
>
> In matrilineal societies, where property, rank, office and group membership are inherited in the female line, it is true that women tend to have greater independence than in patrilineal societies. This is especially so in matrilineal tribal societies where the state has not yet developed, and especially in those tribal societies

where residence is matrilocal – that is, men come to live in the homes or villages of their wives. Even so, in all matrilineal societies for which adequate descriptions are available, the ultimate head of a household, lineage, and local group is usually a man. (Op. cit., p.54.)

Morgan and Engels were probably right in thinking that the human family was preceded by sexual indiscriminacy. They were also right in seeing an egalitarian group-quality about early economic and marriage arrangements. They were without evidence, however, in believing that the earliest mating and economic patterns were entirely group relations. (Op. cit., p.74.)

[In hunting societies]social life is egalitarian. There is of course no state, no organised government. Apart from religious shamans or magicians, the division of labour is based only on sex and age. Resources are owned communally, tools and personal possessions are freely exchanged. Everyone works who can. Band leadership goes to whichever man has the intelligence, courage and foresight to command the respect of his fellows. Intelligent women are also looked up to. (Op. cit., p.63.)

The exploitation of women that came with the rise of the state and of class society will presumably disappear in post-state, classless society – for which the technological and scientific basis already exists.(Op. cit., pp.75-6.)

# APPENDIX

This essay by Steve Drury is from from his *Stepping Stones: The Making of our Home World*, 2016: (https://earthstep.wordpress.com/ebook/). It gives an account of the current evidence from palaeontology/physical anthropology of 'the first human revolution'.

How and when did this first human revolution take place? Until the late twentieth century it was considered to coincide with the first appearance of symbolic art in association with fossil *homo sapiens*, about 100,000 years ago. More recent discoveries by palaeoanthropologists have thrown up many surprising contradictions of that simple notion. They enrich Morgan's seminal insights of 140 years ago into human nature.

Rudimentary stone tools and evidence for their use in butchery of, at first, meaty bones from the kills of big cats, appear in the geological record of East Africa around 3.3 million years ago. Yet neither was found in association with bones of their makers. Yet at that time, East Africa was inhabited by upright hominins (fossils that show both human and ape-like features), the most famous example being 'Lucy', discovered in north-eastern Ethiopia in 1974. Either the species (*Australopithecus afarensis*) to which she belonged or another, undiscovered species, was responsible.

With a brain about the size of a chimpanzee's and standing a little over one metre tall, these beings show three distinctly human characteristics. They walked on two legs. The pelvic bones of females had a much reduced birth canal compared with that of chimpanzee mothers, suggesting delivery of infants at an earlier stage of foetal development and the need for more prolonged parental care than among apes. Significantly, *Australopithecus afarensis* did not have prominent canine teeth, which in modern apes are displayed aggressively by males competing for access to and domination of females. Yet adult males were much larger than females, a feature that is associated with male domination.

Of the several earlier species of hominins none had ape-like canines and all were upright walkers. This evidence indicates a major evolutionary shift in general behaviour among hominins compared with apes since the two groups split and evolved separately. As well as freeing of the hands, male dominance and aggression within hominin bands may have been much reduced; the harbinger of labour and a key requirement for social cooperation.

Around two million years ago, a hominin appeared that resembled modern humans more than it did apes. This was in a butchery site in which remains of *Homo habilis* were found along with crude tools and cut-marked bones of scavenged animals. By 1.9 million years ago, anatomically modern-looking *Homo ergaster* appears in the African fossil record, differing from us only in skull features: a brain half our size; prominent brow ridges; a shallow forehead and lack of a chin. Male and female adults showed about the same size difference as that among modern humans – further evidence for reduced or even vanished dominance of females by males. Armed at first with the same crude tools as their predecessors but an increased brain capacity, members of this species did amazing things.

In a geologically short time, *Homo ergaster* spread throughout habitable Africa and also to Eurasia. At Dmanisi in modern Georgia archaeologists discovered the remains of five individuals in sediments dated between 1.9 and 1.8 million years ago. Within a few hundred thousand years others arrived south of Beijing at latitude 35°N. The Dmanisi hominin skulls are very different from one another, a feature known to occur in small isolated populations when unexpressed genes can manifest themselves in the progeny of close interbreeding.

One skull is that of an elderly woman who had lost all her teeth long before death. She could have survived into old age only with the assistance of her companions – a sign of altruism?

These migrants' descendants survived in Asia until about 30,000 years ago, and, together with *Homo ergaster* in Africa, evolved slightly to new forms, both known as *Homo erectus*. By about 1.6 million years ago the African branch made a fundamental breakthrough in technology and aesthetics. The elegant 'Acheulean' bi-face axe requires days of work by an expert flint knapper to produce a symmetrical blade with one rounded edge that fits perfectly in the hand. For *Homo erectus* in Africa and their successors who migrated into southern Europe, the Middle East and South Asia, and for early modern humans this iconic tool was literally the core of their 'tool kit', which also included means of boring holes, scraping cured skins and cutting meat.

The rock flakes left from axe manufacture show that the tool itself once lay at the core of an irregular block of hard flinty stone. Each was 'liberated' by a maker able to visualise the potential lying within the stone, much as does a modern sculptor. Detailed wear analysis of razor sharp edges shows that a significant number were never used. As well as tools they may have been works of art: items of ritual or objects aimed at attracting partners. The skills required to make them were passed down generations for one and a half million years, from 'species' to 'species' over millions of square kilometres. Regarded by some 'sapiens-centric' anthropologists as indicators of intellectual and cultural stasis, others consider them differently. The possession of a bi-face axe conferred on its user the potential to make a great many other tools, from wood, bone and fibre that soon break down and vanish from the record: possibly the first machine tool!

Asian *Homo erectus* never developed bi-face axes – their ranges lacked hard, flinty stone. In 1891 Eugene Dubois discovered their remains at Trinil in Java, and called them *Pithecanthropus erectus*, suggesting they were Darwin's 'missing link' with anthropoid apes. As well as skull fragments, Dubois collected fossils associated with them. They include freshwater mussel shells dated between 430,000 and 540,000 years ago. In 2016 one of them was found to bear engraved geometric patterns much the same as the earliest art produced by modern humans hundreds of thousand years later.

As well as providing warmth and security from large predators, the use of fire in cooking renders both plant tissue and meat proteins more digestible by the alimentary tract inherited by hominins. The body 'plan' of apes includes a large gut, together with a large belly, capable of digesting raw vegetable matter, and that is a feature of all pre-*Homo* hominins. The earliest full skeleton of *Homo erectus* has the narrow-waisted, barrel-chested shape of all succeeding species of Homo; a major evolutionary change signifying that large digestive tracts were no longer needed. This may have followed the controlled use of fire and cooking, the first known hearth in a South African cave dating back 1.5 million years.

Because of its tenderising effect and release of more nutrition, cooking reduces the time needed to gather and eat sufficient food by about 40 per cent. Use of fire would have encouraged growth of the brain, a major 'consumer' of energy. It would also free time for other productive activities and reflection on the world. Despite their 'primitive' appearance to us, early *Homo erectus* had a basic subsistence strategy little different from that of living hunter gatherers, who have a 'working day' of three to four hours. Evidence for what they did with the spare time is rare, as it is for modern humans before about 40,000 years ago. Unless signs are preserved in hard materials that are not biodegradeable, any trace vanishes quickly.

A qualitative change in the mode of life from instinctive, gene-led interaction with nature to a conscious, socially bound exchange is the essence of the first human revolution. Thereafter humans adopted and adapted natural materials as means of production and sustenance; in changing the world through purposeful labour they changed themselves. Most elements of 'human-ness' had been assembled in *Homo erectus*, almost 2 million years ago. For the first time in Earth's history a land-dwelling species spanned three continents where its members began to express themselves aesthetically.

A fossil skull from the Red Sea lowlands of Eritrea, dated at around 1 million years, has a structure that is intermediate between *Homo erectus* and later humans. Remains of six individuals of this *Homo antecessor*, dated at around 900,000 years, occur jumbled together in a cave in the Atapuerca Mountains of northern Spain. They signify another huge migration that may have involved crossing the Straits of Gibraltar. The bone assemblage shows signs of defleshing, which some have interpreted as evidence for cannibalism But that view ignores the equally likely possibility of a funerary rite.

Since a million years ago, Europe and Asia have been destinations for several waves of African migrants. Differences in skull shape of successive variants have hitherto been used to separate *Homo antecessor, heidelburgensis, neanderthalensis* and last of all *sapiens*. The second left a collection of 300,000-year-old wooden spears in a German peat deposit. At two metres long, they have the same aerodynamic design as modern tournament javelins. Their makers were 'big-game hunters'. In Africa it is difficult to make such a four-fold species division – through time there seems to be a progressive gradation in skull form from *Homo erectus* to *Homo sapiens*. Resolving the apparent conundrum of several human species living somewhere on Earth at any one time over the last million years became possible with twenty-first-century advances in the extraction and analysis of DNA from ancient bones.

In the course of the last great human migration beginning 130,000 years ago, anatomically modern humans entering Eurasia successfully interbred with at least two more ancient species. These were the Neanderthals and a shadowy group (Denisovans) represented only by a small finger bone that yielded a full DNA sequence. Moreover, it seems that some the genes inherited from these ancestors conferred a number of advantages on their descendants, the most striking being the ability to survive and prosper at high altitudes that Tibetans have inherited from the Denisovans. Africans too carry a part of the genetic make-up of another ancient human, yet to be resolved. The survival of such inheritance – through thousands of generations since males and females of at least four supposedly different 'species' interbred – casts doubt on the validity of that taxonomic concept in the context of humanity.

Beings that consciously set out to change the world inevitably change themselves. Given repeated migration out of Africa and lengthy periods of separation, isolation and sometimes catastrophic reductions in numbers, distinct anatomical differences arise equally inevitably. The almost two million years over which that has happened have witnessed huge, global fluctuations in climate and ecosystems through ten major ice ages separated by periods of warming, together with innumerable shorter but drastic climate shifts.

For small, 'pioneer' bands of all variants of the genus *Homo* to survive migration across alien ecosystems during huge shifts in climate demanded resourceful social cooperation as well as conscious, knowledgeable relations with the rest of the natural world. Protracted infant care required male as well as female members to share parental responsibilities within matrilineal bands, for which the first figurative art bears witness: the 'Venus' figurines from 40,000 to 15,000 years ago, and cruder versions from 200,000 to 350,000 years ago. (Note: there are few, if any, examples of male figurines!) Such social and sexual cohesion implies development of sharing, empathy and altruism, and cultural means of ensuring such bonds were maintained. Evidence for such truly human characteristics goes back a very long time. Moreover, the DNA evidence for interbreeding between different groups signifies the unlikelihood of xenophobia based on physiognomies and physiques that seem very alien indeed to us.

The first human revolution was a product, indeed an integral part of that pulsation of ecological opportunity and severe threat; a refinement or distillation of the potential hidden within a very ancient shift by a social ape to walking on two legs that freed hands. Although clear signs of consciousness appear at each stage, this was not a 'purposeful' revolution but a continual, dialectical interplay between humans and nature. The latest products of this process responded to the last phase of ecological and climatic 'tests' by development of their inherited culture to levels that took them everywhere on Earth before discovering agriculture. Other, earlier lines of human inheritance did not survive the tests, except through becoming part of our own genetic make-up and how it is expressed in practice.

PART II

# ESSAYS ON WOMEN'S EMANCIPATION

### YASSAMINE MATHER

## 1: TAHER AHMADZADEH

TaherAhmadzadeh, a veteran member of Iran's JebhehMelli (National Front – Mossadegh's political coalition) and the Freedom Movement, who became briefly the governor of Khorassan province after the Iranian revolution of 1979, died in early December 2017 in Mashad, northern Iran. Most of the Persian language press inside and outside the country published lengthy obituaries. He had been imprisoned both during the Pahlavi period and after the Islamic Revolution and the obituaries dedicated paragraphs to his sons Massoud and Majid, founders of the SazmaneCherikhayeFadayeeyeKhalgh, OIPFG, who were executed by the Shah's regime, and his youngest son, Mojtaba, a sympathiser of another communist organisation, who opposed armed struggle, killed at the age of 25 by the Islamic Republic.

However almost all of these obituaries failed to mention his daughter Mastoureh Ahmadzadeh, who is still alive, who was a political prisoner of the Shah's regime and became a leading figure of OIPFG, a member of its central committee. The editors, journalists and commentators who remind us every day how they have become 'feminists', the very same people who complain daily about the lack of women ministers in Rouhani's government (as if that would make any difference to a government led by a reformist Shia cleric) wrote about Tater Ahmadzadeh and his three sons but not a word about his daughter. It is almost as if she doesn't exist.

This short piece, based on my memories of Mastoureh (comrade Azam) in Kurdistan and later in France, is to balance that omission. She is alive and well, and I know, being the ultra-modest, self-sacrificing woman that she is, she would not thank me for writing this piece. In her belief one should only write about the life of the Fedayeen after their death. However I am deliberately breaking that rule, in response to a genuine anger felt by many on the Iranian left for the blatant omission of her name in articles written about her father.

Mastoureh's brother Massoud Ahmadzadeh (2 March 1945–4 December 1972), a founding member of the Fedayeen, was a political theorist who with Amir ParvizPouyan believed the deathly silence of the left opposition in Iran after the 1953 CIA coup could and should be broken with a series of armed operations paving the way for the defeat of 'capitalism and the comprador bourgeoisie'.

Irrespective of how we judge this political theory now, the movement they started changed the political scene in Iran in the late 1960s and early 1970s. Massoud, a mathematics student in Tehran university, started a rebellion not just against the Shah's regime, but also against the Tudeh Party, the traditional 'official communist' party in Iran, whose name had become synonymous with compromise and betrayal. It goes without saying that the Soviet Union did not support the Iranian revolutionary movement against the Shah. This official pro-Soviet party was for broad alliances and the 'peaceful road to socialism'.

Of course, to take up arms against the Shah's dictatorship was suicidal, because it was inevitable that a large number of those who did so would be killed – and 13 out of the 19 of what was called the original cell of the Fedayeen died in the fighting and a number of members and supporters were executed later. However, the movement survived. In his writings MassoudAhmadzadeh destroyed the illusion that the 'national bourgeoisie' could have a revolutionary or progressive role in late twentieth-century Iran. Describing the democratic socialist character of the revolution, he wrote: 'Struggle against imperialist domination – i.e. world capitalism – has elements of the struggle with capitalism and therefore elements of the socialist revolution are born in this struggle.'

The defeat of successive military operations, the execution and killing of dozens (some say hundreds) of the group's members did not dampen the enthusiasm of the organisation's supporters, nor did it reduce the number of new recruits. The guerrilla operation at Siahkal1 not only opened a new chapter in the life of the radical left in Iran, but also influenced contemporary Iranian poetry and literature beyond the imagination of those who launched it. Mohamad Reza ShafieKadkani's famous poem 'MojKhazar' (written for Siahkal) was memorised by tens of thousands, the event and the subsequent moment made its mark even in pop songs. And, in typical Shia tradition, young Iranians found Marxist martyrs to admire, as opposed to Shia martyrs.

Mastoureh Ahmadzadeh was a member of the central committee of a political organisation which no longer believed in military struggle as 'a tactic and strategy', an organisation that by February 1979 had mass support. Its intervention on 11 February challenged the peaceful transition to power envisaged by Khomeini when OIPFG supporters in the Iranian air force, helped by the group's ability to distribute arms expropriated from military garrisons amongst ordinary people, overwhelmed the Shah's loyal guards in street fights. In the words of Khomeini's first premier, Bazargan: 'We wanted rain, we got floods.' Its meetings in the first few weeks after the February uprising could easily gather half a million members and supporters in Tehran alone.

Even then, many amongst OIPFG's members did believe in arming the working class with the kind of organisation and politics necessary for the overthrow of capitalism in Iran. In the weeks before the Shah's overthrow the group had intensified its work amongst oil workers in Tehran and in the oil regions of the south. These were very different times from Siahkal and one of the leading figures of that period was Mastoureh Ahmadzadeh, recently released from prison. As far as I know, she has only ever written two short pieces about herself. Here is one of them:

> From childhood, my father [TaherAhmadzadeh] had been imprisoned many times, and behind prison doors I was a witness to arrest and torture. I myself was arrested and jailed in Mahshad for the first time for engaging in a strike. The place was not foreign to me. After a while, in the new prison, I lifted the mattress, and found the imprint of Evin on it. I had heard of Evin many times. The prison had been established during TeimourBahktiar's tenure; it was located in the village of Evin; the locale had been turned into a dreadful place of imprisonment. It was one of the worst torture chambers of the SAVAK2. But I had no fear. I had done nothing wrong. Additionally, in those days, being incarcerated on political grounds was an honour. I always asked myself why men were the only ones who were kept in prison. In Mashad prison, they released all of us and only kept the men.3

OIPFG named her their candidate in the elections to the Council of Experts (which replaced the promised Constitutional Assembly) and although no one expected a seat for the left in what became a council full of Shia clerics, the election gave the organisation the opportunity to explain its politics and organise large meetings in major cities.

At the time of the Minority-Majority split in the Fedayeen, the question asked by many of the organisation's supporters was: where does Mastoureh stand? This was partly because details of the political differences were not clear. Rumours, claims and counter claims dominated. That was why many supporters had to decide on the basis of where particular comrades stood vis-à-vis the split. As later became clear, on the whole the opponents of the Islamic Republic were in the Minority faction of the central committee, while the Majority were supporters of the Imam's (Khomeini's) line. Soon after the split it became clear that the Majority was opposing the basic stance taken by MassoudAhmadzadeh and Amir ParvizPouyan in opposing not just the 'reformist/revisionist' position of Tudeh, but also the Soviet Union. The founders of the Fedayeen had no illusions in the 'socialist camp', yet the only justification the Majority could find for giving 'critical support' to the Islamic Republic government was the fact that – despite brutal repression, waging war on Kurdistan and Turkman Sahra and suppressing workers' strikes – the new Islamic regime had moved Iran out of the influence of the United States and closer to the 'socialist camp'. Of course, even this turned out to be an illusion when, a few years later, the regime unleashed its repression on its former supporters, the Tudeh and the Fedayeen Majority.

On this issue, and as far as the domination of the Tudeh line in sections of the Fedayeen was concerned, in my recollection Mastoureh was considering writing a critique of another Fedayeen theorist, Jazani, whose theory of a united front against the Shah's dictatorship could have paved the way for the development of a reformist tendency. Historians might see this as a valid argument.

In any case, at the time of the Majority-Minority split, her opinions on the Tudeh and the Islamic regime were already known. So deciding what faction you support on the basis of Mastoureh's stance was not as silly as it might appear now. In terms of supporters and members, the Minority managed to become the larger of the two groups as students and workers opposed the soft positions taken by the central committee of the organisation vis-à-vis the increasingly repressive Islamic Republic. For many it was the Majority's increasingly pro-government positions and the repetition of slogans we had heard so many times before from Tudeh: 'Iran's revolution is a defeat for the imperialist camp and therefore a victory for the socialist camp'. Those of us who had seen in the writings of Amir ParvizPouyan and MassoudAhmadzadeh the birth of a completely new revolutionary movement couldn't believe what we were reading.

The first time I met Mastoureh Ahmadzadeh was on the first morning I woke up in Baghcheh base of the Fedayeen Minority in Iranian Kurdistan. She had spent most of the night at yet another lengthy central committee meeting. That was the norm, and central committee meetings got longer as time went on, sometimes lasting more than 20 hours with short breaks.

Comrade Azam, as she was called in Kurdistan, looked very tired but enthusiastic. Early in the morning she was ready for a stint as a doctor/GP in a house in the village called 'the clinic'. I was to follow her. She then did her house calls, seeing patients, giving out medications before returning to the base to write her articles. At the time she was editor of the organisation's paper *Kar*. This was followed by more political meetings.

What distinguished her from other members of the central committee was her humility. Unlike the men, who were obviously too busy or too important to take their turn in kitchen and cleaning duties, she seemed to be doing more of these chores than most ordinary residents of the camp, covering for those who were not well, those who had been injured in fighting ... and she worked harder than everyone else in the team in terms of volunteering for the more difficult tasks. Cooking food in large pots over a wood fire or washing dozens of dishes in the river, where the water was already cold in September, were not easy tasks. She also acted as the hairdresser – we lived close to stables and hygiene demanded short hair. On my second day in the camp she informed me that she would cut my hair short, and she did a very good job.

A woman of no airs and graces, she wore the worst pishmarga uniform of all those present. We all wore pishmarga trousers and tops, but hers seemed to be made of poor quality material, and often her top was a different colour to her trousers. A real contrast to another central committee member who seemed to wear an impeccably tailored white pishmarga uniform every day. Later in my stay in Kurdistan I realised 'leaders' such as Jalal Talebani, who I met months later, took great care of their pishmarga uniforms even in the midst of fighting. The uniform was a sign of 'importance'.

In the Baghcheh base, women pishmargas all slept in a room in the school that was acting as our main headquarters. Mastoureh always had the worst place for sleeping. Arriving later than anyone else, she almost invariably slept near the door in a sleeping bag and was up before the rest of us. She was proud of her clinic and took great pleasure showing me around the place. Her pet hate was the fact that some pishmargas had used the alcohol she kept for medical purposes to make spirits – the first and only time I heard a hint of anger in her voice.

A few weeks after my arrival she told me I could go with her to a couple of neighbouring villages while she visited some patients. We went in a jeep and as we approached one of our destinations I could see there was a queue outside a building. By that stage I was not naive enough to think supporters of our political line had gathered there, but as we got off the jeep it became clear they were all waiting for Mastoureh. Word of mouth had informed patients in a number of neighbouring villages that the female doctor was running a clinic and they had come from afar. What impressed me most was her humanity in dealing with her patients. This very busy political leader, editor of a paper, had time for every one of the patients young and old. She comforted the relatives and gave medical advice. And it was all so different from the attitude of other members of the organisation, many of whom were in our base preparing for a plenum.

A French reporter arrived one day, keen to interview her. I did some translation, although her English was very good. The interviewer wanted to know how she felt as a woman in the leadership of a left-wing group. She replied she hadn't felt discrimination in her family or in the organisation, where 'comrades were judged according to their abilities and their efforts'; and then she concentrated on talking about her politics. I don't know if she has changed her mind since then, but in her case it was true that she had moved up in the ranks purely on merit. Mastoureh's record is unique. A political prisoner of the Shah's era, many women political prisoners of different political persuasions remember her as someone who never showed weakness and, of course, as a prisoner who was useful because of her medical training. She was a competent organiser during the year of semi-open activity in Tehran after February 1979, an excellent public speaker and a compassionate Marxist. I am sure the fact that she was the sister of the organisation's founding member was not forgotten by most, but none of this should take away her own qualities and competence.

As a woman who could hide under hijab and chador (a long veil covering the entire body) she was the only member of the central committee who could travel regularly from Kurdistan to Tehran. During my short few months in Baghcheh, before I moved to another base, she undertook the journey to Tehran twice. This was no ordinary journey. Every military checkpoint on the 550- kilometre route, every security post, had large photos of her amongst the most wanted opponents of the Islamic Republic. Yet she could cross those posts wearing contact lenses as opposed to her bespectacled 'wanted' photo, and wearing Islamic clothes. Under her clothes she was carrying articles, leaflets, and organisational instructions for cells in Tehran and elsewhere, all taped to her body.

The morning of her journeys to Tehran you could feel the fear amongst everyone who was staying and of course whoever was travelling with her. What if she got arrested? What if a revolutionary guard recognised her? The only one who seemed at ease, composed and totally fearless was Mastoureh herself. She smiled, joked, and tried to convince others that there would be no problem. The return journey from Tehran was just as dangerous; she was bringing reports from the cells and committees in Tehran and other cities, issues of regional papers, penicillin and painkillers.

In retrospect, a few months later, we came to realise these were the good times. That winter, the base in Baghcheh hosted the much delayed plenum, while mourning the terrible death of 12 Fedayeen fighters caught in a trap set by Islamic Revolutionary Guards. By that time I was in another base but I could imagine how it must have affected everyone in Baghcheh. This was the start of the worst period in the history of the Fedayeen in Iranian and later Iraqi Kurdistan. Spiralling internal conflict in the absence of open discussion led to one disaster after another and, of course, as a member of the central committee Mastoureh Ahmadzadeh does accept responsibility for many of the political and organisational mistakes of that period. However, historians looking at that particular period, where left-wing Iranian opposition groups were caught in a war zone between Iran's Islamic Republic and Iraq's Saddam Hussein, will probably take a more sympathetic view of her actions.

The next time I saw Mastoureh was in Paris, when the second congress of OIPFG, delayed for many years because of logistic but also political reasons, was being organised. The three surviving members of the central committee had fallen out with each other. If you saw them in a room together, as I did during my visits, you could tell that the political and personal animosity was so severe that nothing could save the group from splits.

Yet as the two male members of the central committee were busy leaking information to allies and cells under their responsibility, gossiping and spreading false rumours about their opponents, she did not utter a word against fellow central committee members, she did not divulge any organisational secret until the day she resigned. For those of us who could see her pain and wanted to help it was impossible to get her to break her own rigid rules: when it came to democratic centralism she did not waver from her principles one millimetre.

Gossiping, making false accusations against political opponents is not her style. For her, democratic centralism wasn't some superficial idea you talked about in order to impress lower ranks. At the worst period of her political life, as she saw the organisation that meant so much to her being destroyed, she remained calm and in control of her emotions, she did not betray her own standards.

But all through this time the men of the central committee were busy telling everyone that as an emotional woman she wasn't thinking straight and that is why she wasn't choosing their faction against the other one. The reality was she no longer trusted either of them. Despite her unassuming and modest attitude, even after her resignation from the central committee and the organisation – just before a split that saw its complete demise – she had by far the largest number of supporters in what was left of the Fedayeen inside and outside the country.

After all she had endured, the last straw must have been facing threats to her life a few years later by those she had considered fellow comrades. But even then when I met her in Paris, at a time when many of us worried about her safety and her life, she remained unaffected by all the fuss, concentrating on her own work.

Of course none of this matters to mainstream Iranian feminists (male or female) who concentrate on the career prospects of professional women. These days the dominant feminist discourse is used by neoliberal capital to justify the exploitation of the working class in a globalised economy. What matters are measures that allow middle-class and upper-class women to progress in the political, economic and social spheres, yet the effect of such measures on the day-to-day life of working-class women is more problematic, often negative.

In the era of individualistic, neoliberal feminism, why should anyone bother about women such as Mastoureh Ahmadzadeh – she isn't the CEO of a company, she is not a minister, she is not the daughter of a famous ayatollah. Her extraordinary life is not even worth recognition of her existence in obituaries of her father. Yet for some of us, she remains the very embodiment of what was revolutionary, courageous and principled in the old OIPFG.

## NOTES

(NB: all websites cited were last accessed on 15 April 2018.)

1. At Siahkal on the Caspian Sea, on 8 February 1971, Fedayeen guerrillas attacked a gendarmerie post, killing three policemen and freeing two arrested guerrillas. Thirteen men were convicted and executed for the incident, including two who were in prison at the time.

2. SAVAK , the Shah's brutal secret police force.

3. FaribaAmini, 'Cries from the heart: history of torture and abuse of women in Iranian prisons': http://www.payvand.com/news/06/oct/1239.html

# 2: NEOLIBERAL FEMINISM

## *SEXIST SOCIETY*

One reason why guerrilla organisations have a better record of combating sexism is because they are isolated from society. Their members do not interact within normal society. The claim that Fedayeen women activists of the 1980s were totally 'liberated' must be taken with a pinch of salt. However, there is no doubt that separation from day-to-day family tasks did present unparalleled 'opportunities' for women. We live in a patriarchal society and removal from it at least presents us with the possibility of creating conditions where sexism can be more easily combated.

By definition guerrilla women did not have household responsibilities. Either we were childless or those with children had their offspring looked after by parents or relatives in cities and villages far from the battlefield. We did not have any gender-specific duties, so, in that respect, living in a collective military base was to a very limited extent like living in post-revolutionary conditions. Female comrades in European left-wing organisations (maybe with the exception of a few full-timers) spend the majority of their time in a sexist environment – as wage-earners (often on lower wages than their male counterparts), as carers for children and the elderly, as unpaid workers doing housework (and, in the vast majority of cases, spending many more hours on housework than the men they live with). At the best of times it would be impossible to expect a political organisation to deal with the day-to-day discrimination women activists face in society – discrimination unrelated to party activity.

To overcome this situation there are difficult personal, social and political choices to be made and in my opinion those who put politics in command often come out of it stronger. As women, we may vent all our frustrations about sexual inequality within the political organisations to which we belong. It is certainly easy to play the role of the victim, but for a revolutionary such attitudes are cop-outs. If we are to combat sexism within our organisations, we must start by building female comrades' self-confidence.

Women activists are often their own worst enemy when it comes to their own capabilities, organisationally and politically. On this issue we must rebel against stereotyped work. We need to consider the possibility of ditching housework and reducing care duties so that we have enough time to write articles, to participate in meetings, to organise. But many female comrades are not in a position to do so – who would look after their children? Who would care for their elderly parent? Some do not want to do so, yet all of us expect miracles from our political organisation.

### *PHYSICAL AND MENTAL*

Even guerrilla organisations take note of the fact that there are physical differences between men and women, and some tasks are more suited to women's physical capabilities.

However, life in a combat zone leaves little room for chivalry. Women might be issued with lighter guns and in the case of the Fedayeen, female combatants had to come to terms with the company of a dedicated male bodyguard, who would have his gun pointed to her head when they ventured into dangerous areas. This bizarre custom was meant to ensure that the organisation would never allow a female fighter to fall into the hands of the Islamic regime. Upon arrival in Kurdistan, my immediate reaction to this practice was to condemn it as an insult. But a few weeks into my stay, having heard about the kind of torture Islamic Guards reserved for communist women, I actually found it reassuring that my bodyguard would make sure I was dead rather than taken prisoner. It was a practical step taken to deal with a specific issue.

However, with the exception of this single practice, men and women wore the same uniform, performed the same tasks, were treated more or less equally in the camp, in battle and in the division of labour.

In Kurdistan, maybe because we lived so far from reality (away from capitalist commodity fetishism, away from the false modesty imposed by the Shia state) our appearance seemed to have no significance and this in itself had a liberating effect. Qualities such as the ability to debate, organise and, yes, shoot accurately, were considered far more important than looks – our military uniform did not leave much room for coquetry. Both in Kurdistan and later as the representative of the organisation abroad, I was well aware that using make-up and spending time on one's appearance in other ways were considered serious flaws.

I know this will be frowned upon by modern feminists, but if revolutionary women are to be equal with men there must come a time when we stop becoming victims of commodity fetishism – a time when we refuse to be concerned about our appearance. Apart from anything else, this will leave us more time for politics, its theory and practice. Whether we like it or not, the inequality in terms of the time we spend on non-political tasks – be it family, housework, childcare or our appearance – does contribute to our lack of confidence. It does make us victims of a sexist culture, sexist society. It is up to us individually and collectively to change this: we cannot expect men to do it for us.

Communists recognise the double burden of oppression, relating to production and reproduction, suffered by women in class society – and we struggle to end it. For us the fight for women's emancipation is an integral part of the struggle for socialism. It is indeed one of the many reasons why we fight for a classless society.

Having said that, it would be utterly wrong to suggest that we might as well forget about women's struggles under capitalism and wait for socialism. We fight in the here and now for demands that will improve the lot of working-class women and for genuine social, political and economic equality.

Yet the majority of the left (both in advanced capitalist and developing countries) have been duped by formal, often ineffective forms of gender equality. They are quick to praise the adoption of such superficial 'equality' measures that appear to favour women's participation in social and political life, but in reality are nothing more than an integral part of 'cultural capitalism'.1 In other words 'global capitalism with a human face'.

Over the last two to three decades capitalism has succeeded in convincing many that formal equality, mainly benefiting upper-middle-class and upper-class women, is the same as genuine equality for all. Most rational human beings oppose obvious injustice, and modern capitalism has been able to use such emotional responses to its benefit, concealing the class character of inequality (especially when it comes to gender inequality) through superficial measures and short cuts. Slavoj Zizek has argued that cultural capitalism 'short-circuits' the emotional process by championing the 'charitable act'. I would say the entire quota system is part of this form of 'charitable act'.

Far from helping those affected by discrimination, cultural capitalism is actually harmful to the people it claims to benefit, mainly because it fails to mention the causes of inequality, never mind addressing those causes. It relies on cheap sentiment and plays on guilt.

In the words of Peter Suechting of the blog AC Voice: 'Our involvement in cultural capitalism is, in fact, the most maddening of all its injustices: it involves every one of us in its immorality, making every one of us guilty, without our knowledge or explicit approval, just through naive participation.'2

## *FINANCIALISATION*

Let me start then with identity politics and intersectionality, in order to explain what they are and how they have influenced the issues of quotas, and positive and negative discrimination.

I think it is fair to say that if you live in the academic world or if you have spent time with students or staff in some faculties, you might come to the conclusion that the whole issue of identity politics has become the 'hegemonic theory of our time'. Of course, this is not true of the rest of society, even though we hear a lot about identity politics and to a certain extent the issues arising from them influence policy-making in the public sector.

To understand the politics of identity we have to look at capitalism, and how contemporary modes of production and social relations, as well as reproduction, have changed since the 1970s; we have to understand that these changes have been as influential as women's liberation, the events of 1968, black movements, gay liberation and so on.

It is true that identity politics and intersectionality came as a response to second-wave feminism. Second-wave feminism looked at production in terms of labour relations, but also at reproduction and women's rights. By reproduction, I do not mean just childbirth, but housework and women's tasks regarding the family's physical and mental health. Both of these relations have dramatically changed in advanced capitalist countries. Despite gains made by women during the Second World War, in the post-war decades capitalism continued to rely on a gendered division of labour. If the woman went to work, she remained solely responsible for housework, while the main breadwinner was still the man. That division created a very clear demarcation between productive and reproductive roles.

This gender separation was manifested in the whole of society, not just in the family. For example, during the daytime you would not see many men on the streets: it was the women who were out doing the shopping and so on. It is true that the 'nuclear family' was confronted by many changes in the 1970s – I do not underestimate the influence of the women's movement, the other liberation movements, 1968 and so on. But what was happening beneath all this was western capitalism's financialisation – moving away from domestic production and towards the transfer of industries to where there was cheaper labour and an absence of workers' rights, presenting fewer obstacles to the maximum extraction of surplus value. At the same time, we were seeing the advance of women's liberation, the advent of the pill, the sexual freedoms of the late 1960s and so on. The combination of these two created a particular situation – in some ways a very important phase in the change of the structure of the family. As casualisation and contracted, short-term labour increased, women gained employment and became part of the workforce, while at the same time what were regarded as male jobs were being lost and unemployment amongst men grew. So we had, on the one hand, a change in social relations and, on the other, political change resulting from the demands of the liberation movements, at the same time as the economy was being transformed in most advanced capitalist countries.

In this situation capitalism was able to use the ideas of the liberation movements to its benefit, overseeing superficial changes in terms of gender without addressing the fundamental causes of inequality. There is no reason why surplus value should only be extracted from one gender and its extraction from women had a specific rationale: by focusing on inequality in terms of the individual woman, class oppression was obscured. For identity politics, society became a collection of individuals, or social groups with natural characteristics. These were not based on their economic or class position, but on their gender, race or sexual orientation. In this way, identity politics took over what were the remnants of the left within the women's liberation movement, which separated itself from class struggles and became engulfed in an individualistic, or 'personalised', version of struggle.

## *INTERSECTIONALITY*

It was in this situation that intersectionality – the study of intersections between forms or systems of oppression, domination or discrimination, for example black feminism – came to address the shortcomings of identity politics, by talking of the autonomous struggles of gendered, radicalised sections of labour. In addition we saw the development of radical movements that took into consideration the black power, LGBT and women's movements. By the mid- to late 1970s, they were also functioning as critiques of the 'western labour aristocracy', which had, under Keynesianism, become part of the establishment, according to these views.

I do not think this was simply a reflection of 'Maoist spontaneity'. The left in Europe and North America was paying attention to the Third World, and was concerned about issues of racial and sexual inequality, while the labour aristocracy, a beneficiary of Keynesian economics, was no longer interested in radical forms of struggle. It is, of course, essential for the left to champion the struggles of the most oppressed. In the US racial segregation applied to jobs, while in Northern Ireland skilled jobs were only for Protestant workers. So there was some justification in terms of intersectionality when the left argued that in specific circumstances it was fighting for black workers rather than just 'workers'. The problem arose when this became the dominant discourse.

Sections of the left were primarily concerned with women's, black and gay rights, at a time when the workers' movement was being successfully attacked in terms of anti-union legislation, the removal of services and welfare and in terms of the strengthening of free market ideology and impact of neoliberalism. However, the state could respond to these demands for gender/race equality, dilute their class content and divert the movement into individualism. Capitalism's dual oppression of women remained in place. Obviously it was not going to divert resources to free childcare, cooperative kitchens or care of the elderly.

Women were told that they were free to work, that they were liberated from the shackles of the nuclear family – there was some truth in that – but at the same time they had no additional support as they took up full-time or part-time work. The double burden of oppression – production and reproduction – remained. Capitalism was able to benefit in a number of ways: sections of the labour force had to accept lower wages for part-time, contract employment at a time when blue-collar, skilled employment for men was being undercut.

The arguments about intersectionality, which developed quite considerably in the United States, emphasised the politics of difference: gender, race, sexuality. Within this developed the idea that the most oppressed would make the most militant and therefore the best leaders. This in my view is a completely mistaken idea. First of all, the most oppressed will not necessarily become the most class-conscious. There is no direct correlation between the two. By the late 1980s and 1990s, as the attack on labour continued, as we approached the era of the 'end of history', the era of 'there is no alternative', capitalism had absorbed and incorporated some of the demands of the women's movement and to a certain extent those of the black, anti-racist movement too.

Capitalism appeared victorious: it seemed to have won the ideological argument. It is precisely during this period that a significant part of the women's liberation movement became part of the status quo, part of the system. The absence of major class battles aided this process. This is not to say that the demands put forward by the women's movement were secondary – any principled working-class organisation would have to embrace them. And it is not true that we are all just workers, so we are all the same. If you were a black female cleaner at that time then quite clearly you were different from a white skilled worker. Different forms of oppression demand specific slogans, specific programmatic demands. But the idea that in the absence of fundamental systemic change such oppression can be removed through intersectionality is foolish indeed.

There is no doubt that capitalism has no problem with the extraction of surplus value from women. It can benefit from the employment of a cheap female workforce, which in times of high male unemployment accepts casual, low-paid work. However, this has nothing whatsoever to do with gender equality. Yet capitalism has convinced large sections of the female population that they have achieved such equality, because the most obvious forms of gender discrimination have gone, because they are free to go out to work. What is forgotten is that often this formal equality has been achieved at the expense of increased poverty, of greater exploitation.

But such superficiality has its attractions. It fuels support for the idea that 'if only we could get equal representation then everything would be fine'. This, together with individualism, has played a significant part in the acceptance of the quota system as a means of promoting women alongside men.

## *'EQUALITY'*

Most of my arguments so far have been about the use of a corporate ideology to fool the many. This has had its effect in both the public and private sector.

Positive discrimination is more prominent in the public sector, but in the private sector too anti-discrimination measures are overseen by 'equality officers' who are supposed to monitor and ensure the implementation of equality legislation. In the public sector job applicants are asked to supply information about their gender, sexuality and race. Of course, you can opt out of answering particular questions, but the system has advanced beyond the formal approach. In any case, are you, for example, going to admit you are gay if you are applying for a post where staff are likely to be predominantly male and possibly homophobic? When it comes to the interview panel, it should whenever possible include a woman and a person of colour – although the token woman may often be tougher on members of her own sex than her male counterparts. The main purpose of such procedures is to protect the public sector from legal challenge, and in reality prejudices remain and selection processes have not changed that much.

So this formal, legalistic approach creates the illusion of dealing with equality, but often it results in new means of protecting discrimination.

Women face sexism on a daily basis at work, be it in the form of cheap, prejudiced comments or in the form of an unwillingness to employ pregnant women or those with young children, who are classified as unreliable. So, although we have the appearance of equality, in reality it is mainly formal.

Having said that, when we are arguing against quotas there is a danger in saying that it is because we want the 'best' person for the post. The reason I am saying this is that 'best' is an ambiguous word – best for whom? On what level? It brings with it elements of the liberal meritocracy. When it comes to left-wing politics, we should judge comrades in terms of their class-consciousness, their radicalism in defending the working class irrespective of gender, sexuality or race. But that is different from arguing against quotas in terms of personal characteristics – we should put politics in command.

The whole quota system presents a danger when you specify the number of women or members of national minorities you want on this or that committee. You are accepting, perhaps unconsciously, that the politics of the gay black man/woman do not matter – she/he is the most oppressed, and the most oppressed is the 'best militant'.

In terms of race, the quota system has been introduced into many institutions, particularly in the United States. Of course, we have had the first black president, and earlier Colin Powell was the top military figure. But recently I came across a book explaining how the US military in Vietnam had used racial quotas for its officers in order to reduce tensions amongst soldiers. The first thing that came into my mind when I read this was, what would I think if I was being carpet-bombed? 'Isn't it great that the officer giving the orders is an African-American'?

You could make similar points about gender quotas. Lloyds Bank recently announced that it is changing its approach, since some of its strategies had been 'too aggressive' in the past. The new policy is for more women executives on the board, because they will create the framework for less aggressive banking.3You can really see this working when someone who cannot pay their mortgage goes to their branch to ask for an extension or relaxation of the terms. The bank will obviously show more understanding (and be less concerned about the effect on its profits) now that it has become feminised!

In fact the opposite is likely to occur. When capitalism places women in positions of power, it 'masculinises' them – whatever their personal characteristics, such positions will impose ruthlessness and callousness upon them. We live, after all, in a capitalist, misogynistic society. Its essence remains the same: only the superficial appearance has changed. And because such 'equality' is based on individualism, because there is no class content to it, there is little which unites this layer of privileged figures – the female Lloyds board member or the black US military commander – with the ordinary people of their sex or race. In fact the gap is much bigger than that between a working-class man and woman or a black man and woman. For instance, the Institute for Public Policy Research has published a report under the headline 'Elitist feminism failed working-class women'. It stated that the pay differential amongst women is much more substantial than between men and women.

## *GLASS CEILING*

In contrast to this superficial equality, the writings of revolutionary feminists such as Alexandra Kollontai, Clara Zetkin and so on are concerned with fundamental change. Sometimes we can see a glimmer of such a society in, say, a mining village during a militant strike or a liberated zone in an occupied country, where the norms of class rule have temporarily broken down and the expectations of women have changed for the better.

The difference with the current reality is that there is, on the one hand, formal equality, but, on the other, the continuation of dual oppression, made worse by low-paid jobs and all the rest, and this can be quite difficult to cope with: in fact many women cannot cope with it. Single working-class mothers in particular are often impoverished despite being in work – and they have all the reproductive, domestic and childcare work as well.

And then there are those who say, 'We've given you equality, but you're still not doing very well, are you?' Women have access to higher education and to the top jobs, but very few of them actually make it. So there must be something wrong with them, or maybe they just aren't as ambitious as men. That is the logical corollary of the quota-based individualistic approach. The misogynists have drawn their own conclusions from this constant obsession with the gender 'glass ceiling'.

The argument is, of course, that, since women make up 50 per cent of the population, 50 per cent quotas for all responsible positions will make the relevant organisation more representative. It was this thinking that lay behind New Labour's all-women short lists for the selection of MPs.

But things are never that simple. The majority of women will be unable to 'accept the opportunity' provided by quotas because of their personal circumstances. The double burden has not, after all, been abolished, so can they accept an additional workload when they are already struggling to juggle paid employment with housework and childcare? Some of those who agree to apply for a particular post just to make up the quota may do so reluctantly. Many of 'Blair's babes' – those who benefited from women-only short lists and were able to become MPs – confess that once in parliament they did not like to focus too much on women's issues (which, remember, they were meant to be there to champion), suspecting that this would not be the best way to advance their political careers.

Academic studies analysing the impact of quota systems may measure their 'success' in terms of the number of women now taking up the positions that have been opened up. Yet their findings are often discouraging for supporters of the new arrangements. For example, in a book called *The Impact of Gender Quotas*(OUP, 2012), Susan Franceschet, Mona Lena Krook and Jennifer M Piscopo came to the conclusion that women's symbolic presence does little to increase overall political interest and participation. That is in line with other findings, which have concluded that women's quotas had no 'trickle-down' effect when it came to political activity and did little in terms of attracting others to follow the example of the 'role models'.

Despite all this, those within the women's movement who have accepted the structures and the legal, political and economic existence of capital continue to champion quota-based 'gender balance' on company boards and in political parties. We were constantly told that things would change for the better as a result, that the system would become more humane. Nothing could be further from the truth. The economic infrastructure has not changed, and political and cultural prejudices persist. Under such circumstances the exercise was bound to fail.

A study in Norway, where companies are required to appoint female directors and board members, is interesting, as it shows the shallowness of such approaches. Sabina Tacheva and Morten Huse, in a paper entitled *Women Directors and Board Task Performance: Mediating and Moderating Effects of Board Working Style* (ResearchGate 2006) summarise a conclusion shared by many other studies of the Norwegian experience: 'Minority directors are less likely to be well connected in the managerial world and need to engage in an ingratiation behaviour in order to be appointed to corporate boards.' Women directors are often appointed not for their existing contacts and membership of business networks, but rather for their acquaintance with the CEO or other senior figure: 'Hence, women directors are less likely to effectively perform their service task, and boards with female members are less linked to the firm's external environment, have less access to critical external resources and are therefore less efficient in their service task than homogeneous boards composed of only male directors.

## *NO SOLUTION*

My next example of a system of positive discrimination comes from Iran's Islamic Republic. In Iran the families of the 'martyrs' of the Iran-Iraq war (1980-88) that took the lives of half a million Iranians benefit from positive discrimination. They get special consideration when it comes to entering university, applying for medical insurance, buying a car ... But, over the years, these measures have caused resentment, especially amongst youth. Students who have studied hard but cannot enter university are angry that their places are taken by a relative of a *janbaz*(martyr), who has not even sat the entrance exam. However, the beneficiaries are not particularly happy either. They often complain of the way fellow students dismiss or play down their achievements, even when they do well during their university course.

In this there is a parallel with critiques of quota systems in academia. Women who work hard or who have a strong commitment, and are therefore able to advance, are judged alongside those who have been given privileged treatment and their work is downgraded as a result.

In Norway, the only country where there are regulations governing the number of women on company boards, those who have actually been appointed on merit are numbered among the 'golden skirts' – those who are there just to make up the quota. Similarly, Amy Wallace, a journalist who created a campaign called Women Eds We Love, is very clear on this point in her own area of work: 'Women editors don't want to be judged or rewarded for their gender.4

And quotas in left-wing organisations may often have the effect of devaluing the actual achievement of women comrades who work as hard as, or harder than, their male counterparts. These women are striving to represent the interests of the working class, not looking for the prestige of a more senior position, but the quota system conflates these two outlooks.

There is the additional problem that very often women promoted as a result of quotas are quite subservient to the authority that has put them in that position. There is good empirical evidence to show that they are less questioning of authority, less questioning of the existing political structures. In terms of the left they are often less questioning of the leadership, even if they are part of the central committee, because they have been incorporated, they feel a sense of gratitude and loyalty – an obligation to not rock the boat.

There is a well-known example of this from the Iranian left, where the quota system employed meant that half the central committee had to be women. However, because many were regarded as being there just to make up the numbers, their views were not properly considered. That resulted in the effective establishment of two parallel bodies: the official central committee and the real central committee, which met, discussed and produced actual policy, completely divorced from its impotent twin.

All these examples demonstrate the dangers of a policy that merely addresses surface appearances rather than the actual reality. It may be adopted with good intentions, but cannot deliver if it continues to operate within a deeply unequal, misogynist framework, leaving its substance untouched. Neoliberal capitalism has incorporated demands for equality in respect of gender, race and sexuality and in the process robbed them of their radical content. The empirical data provided from within the system shows that this approach cannot work.

The same applies to the use of quotas within left-wing organisations. They will not just result in the kind of practical problems I have mentioned, but in the long term their adoption can actually harm the cause of women's liberation – the bad examples can be used to reinforce discriminatory practices, to 'prove the validity' of misogynistic ideas.

I am realistic enough to accept that arguing against quotas may not be broadly accepted on the left. But I do not think that succumbing to neoliberal 'cultural capitalism' is the solution.

## NOTES

1. The term 'cultural capital' was used by Pierre Bourdieu and Jean-Claude Passeron. Slavoj Žižek has used 'cultural capitalism' to refer to ethical consumption, as a solution to global problems. I would add 'ethical campaigns for equality' to the list.

2. Peter Suechting, 'Global Capitalism with a Human Face?', *AC Voice*, December 2012: http://acvoice.com/2012/12/02/global-capitalism-with-a-human-face

3. 'Lloyds bank group pledges to employ more women', BBC News, 3 February 2014: www.bbc.co.uk/news/business-26011447

4. See Amy Wallace News: www.amy-wallace.com/news

# 3: WOMEN AND SAFE SPACES

## *SOCIALIST WOMEN MUST OPPOSE BOURGEOIS ATTEMPTS TO IMPOSE 'SAFE SPACES'*

Socialists should be in the forefront of the battle for the emancipation of the oppressed. So they should and do struggle against misogyny, racism and homophobia – not just as an integral part of the struggle for socialism, but also in support of women, minorities and gays against the burden of double oppression under capitalism. How can we do otherwise, given the obvious fact that 50 per cent of the population are women and we live in multinational, multicultural societies?

So the debate in the left and my disagreements with so-called 'safe spaces' has always been about one issue: how can we best achieve this aim? How can we find revolutionary ways of confronting misogyny, homophobia, etc within our own ranks and in society? Such a task cannot be undertaken if we limit ourselves to formal, often ineffective, forms of gender equality proposed by neoliberal capital – policies that are an integral part of 'cultural capitalism', in other words, 'global capitalism with a human face'. We cannot rely on capitalist legal frameworks, regulations and 'safeguards', often produced to do the opposite of what they claim.

Most of the lengthy legislation in the health service, schools, universities, social services, care homes regarding 'equality' and 'safety' is written to protect the relevant organisations from prosecution for neglecting their duty to those in their care or in relation to legislation regarding formal equality. Very often they are not worth the paper they are written on. They are long, complex documents earning money for lawyers, but they rarely relate to real work conditions and should not be duplicated by organisations of the left.

In my opinion such legislation is patronising and bureaucratic.

On the contrary, as adults women need a progressive culture that encourages them and everyone else to challenge sexism, homophobia and racism. Comrades in the left are not weak creatures: they are conscious individuals who recognise capitalism as their enemy – that is why they are in politics. They do not need protective legislation of the type social workers use when dealing with vulnerable children.

Here the example that comes to my mind is the struggles of Iranian women over the last 35 years. They had to fight misogyny not only at home, but in every aspect of social, political and economic life. The state claimed that their 'safety' was best maintained by segregation – in the home, or behind the hijab in the street. But women rejected this from the first days of the Islamic Republic. They took to the streets and fought against misogynist legislation and, although there are still many battles to win, they have made great strides against all odds – to such an extent that the women's movement in Iran is by far the most significant social movement of the region. Would they have been able to achieve this if in their battles against misogyny they had retreated to 'safe spaces'? Of course not. On the contrary, it is precisely the 'safe spaces' provided by the clerical regime that they are rebelling against.

On the left the most effective way to fight sexism and racism is to make sure we battle against privileged positions and the abuse of power, against secrecy and cronyism. It was not lack of safe spaces that led to the disastrous situation in the Socialist Workers Party. It was secrecy, the power of those in authority, their ability to use 'confidentiality' to suppress reporting. A 'safe spaces' policy cannot protect women from a 'comrade Delta'.

## *ACADEMIC DEBATES*

Safe spaces or echo chambers? According to Wikipedia, an echo chamber in the media is 'a situation in which information, ideas or beliefs are amplified or reinforced by transmission and repetition inside an "enclosed" system, where different or competing views are censored or disallowed'. Others have described echo chambers as spaces where people repeat and agree with certain ideas, congratulating each other rather than discussing new, conflicting ideas.

In an echo chamber nobody learns anything new or expands their perspectives. Similarly if women, blacks or LGBTQ activists refuse to confront their opponents, 'safe spaces' risk becoming 'echo chambers'. A 1998 study by Robert Boostrom questions the 'safety' aspect of 'safe spaces' in universities as counterposed to the mission of higher education to promote critical thinking.1 If critical thinking is desirable in higher education, it is essential in a political organisation of the left.

One of the most informative studies about 'safe spaces' in universities has been carried out by Betty J Barrett, published in the *Canadian Journal for the Scholarship of Teaching and Learning*(Vol1/1, February 2010). Under the title, 'Is safety dangerous?',2 Barrett points out a number of theoretical criticisms relating to the construction of educational communities as safe spaces for students, in support of her claim that they may indeed be counterproductive to student learning. She refers to an empirical study by Holley and Steiner ('What is a Safe and an Unsafe Space?' 2005),3 which found that students overwhelmingly 'placed the responsibility for the creation of safety on instructors, listing 387 instructor characteristics that defined safe space. Indeed, the number-one characteristic that students reported as defining a safe learning environment was that the instructor was perceived by students to be non-judgmental and/or unbiased.'

The BBC makes a very similar claim. In a class society faced with many contradictions, how will we identify these figures, so essential to the maintenance of safe spaces, these responsible adults who will remain 'unbiased'? How can we guarantee against abuses of power by such figures themselves in the proposed 'safe space'?

## *STAY AT HOME*

'Safe spaces' must have rules to ensure that the participants know what is acceptable and what is unacceptable. If the participants violate these rules, they are usually warned, removed or blocked. Safe spaces by definition do not tolerate certain 'oppressive' views, but who defines what is oppressive? There clearly cannot be much of a debate about an issue deemed to be oppressive – hence the accusation by some feminists in the US that 'safe spaces are silencing sisterhood', valuing 'safety over debate' and 'leading to a tyranny of silencing and self-censorship, a policy of shutting up debate, keeping any dissent out of their little world."4

The exclusion of trans women from feminist 'safe spaces' has also led to a number of debates challenging the concept of safety:

> In reality, you are only 'safe' from things that might make you uncomfortable or triggered if you stay at home, where you have absolute control over everything that happens (and even then, not always). Each person's idea of 'safe' is different, and therefore a group space cannot possibly be 'safe'. 'Safe' isn't real, and as such I believe it's not worth investing energy in. It's much better, in my opinion, to create spaces where there are a few clear rules for acceptable behaviour (which does not depend on identity or status of any kind, gender or otherwise), a stated expectation of kindness and goodwill, and one or several people who are in charge of smoothing things out if they go wrong.5

We are told safe spaces are places or communities – either online or off – where bigotry and oppressive views are not tolerated. As you can see from the examples above, such a policy creates contradictions, even when applied in a feminist caucus, a classroom, in social work. At best one can say the policy might work for a small sect trying to live in isolation.

Our task is quite different: we intend to change society and we cannot hide from reality. We are socialists because we believe we can change society. We are not in the business of creating cocoons to protect us from evil – we intend to fight and destroy evil. If we are serious about recruiting from the working class, with all its prejudices, we must confront its homophobia, its sexism and its racism. We cannot start from the premise of exclusion.

We are not bourgeois politicians. We openly confront international, national and local evils. More importantly we are not in the business of combating these evils with reform here, legislation there: we want a new kind of society, not just here in Britain, but for the world. That is precisely why in our political activity, in our political organisations, we cannot hide from reality – we cannot and should not seek 'safe spaces'.

We do not believe human beings are born racist or sexist – they are made so by the social conditions they inhabit. We believe that ultimately only a minority whose class interests are served by exploitation, war and destruction will resist change. We are confident in our ability to persuade the majority. We are convinced that the best way to fight nationalism and xenophobia, for example, is to explain the history of colonialism and imperialism to those who have been duped into believing such divisive nonsense. We know that the best way to deal with xenophobia, misogyny or Islamophobia is to confront it head on.

We are not in the business of falsifying reality. We reject the idea that racism and sexism can be fully defeated under capitalism and we refuse to go along with the notion that that we should aim to create little zones free from racism or sexism in an unjust capitalist world. On the contrary, we argue that the system relies on divide and rule, that racism and sexism are by-products of the prevailing economic order. We are not a religious sect that seeks to isolate its members from reality. We are determined to fight the barbarism created by the continued existence of capitalism and it is in this respect that we call ourselves revolutionaries rather than reformists. We believe that better jobs with better pay cannot be achieved by keeping out immigrants.

The problem is capitalism and we see it as our responsibility to explain this to those sections of the working class that blame foreigners for job losses, low wages, poor housing and cuts.

We do not seek to create non-racist zones in impoverished areas, where migrants can be protected from racist or chauvinistic attitudes. We want to change the world, not escape from it. Unlike social workers we do not aim to help workers find individual temporary relief. We are for a collective fight and we need comrades prepared to fearlessly study and discuss questions of history, economics and philosophy, to engage in arduous debate. How can we expect them to do so if they are constantly engaged in self-censorship, if their main concern is to avoid forceful argument for fear of offending others?

## NOTES

1. Robert Boostrom, '"Safe Spaces": Reflections on an Educational Metaphor', *Journal of Curriculum Studies*, vol. 30, no. 4, pp. 397-408 (Jul-Aug 1998).

2. Betty J. Barret, 'Is "Safety" Dangerous? A Critical Examination of the Classroom as Safe Space', *The Canadian Journal for the Scholarship of Teaching and Learning*, vol.1, issue 1, article 9, February 2010: http://ir.lib.uwo.ca/cgi/viewcontent.cgi?article=1005&context=cjsotl_rcacea

3. Vlad Chjou, 'What is a safe and an unsafe space': https://www.academia.edu/16305620/WHAT_IS_A_SAFE_AND_AN_UNSAFE_SPACE

4. Quiet Riot Girl (An Elly Tams Production), 'Safe Spaces, 'Silencing', Sisterhood': http://quietgirlriot.wordpress.com/2011/03/29/safe-spaces-silencing-sisterhood

5. Sexgeek, 'if trans women aren't welcome, neither am I', posted September 20, 2013: http://sexgeek.wordpress.com/2013/09/20/if-trans-women-arent-welcome-neither-am-i